HOOKED RUGS

HOOKED RUGS

An American Folk Art

With Patterns for Ten Rugs to Make

by Leslie Linsley

Photographs by Jon Aron

Clarkson Potter/Publishers

Published by Clarkson N. Potter, Inc.,
201 East 50th Steet, New York, New York 10022.
Member of the Crown Publishing Group.
CLARKSON N. POTTER, POTTER, and colophon are trademarks of
Clarkson N. Potter, Inc.

Manufactured in Japan
Design by Barbara Peck
Photographs on pages 56–57, copyright © 1992 by Doug Mindell; pages 22–23, 52, 58, 63
bottom, 102–103, copyright © 1992 by Daniel P. Smith; 25, 38, 46–47, 54, 65 right, 68–69, 83,
85, 87, 88, 119, 125, copyright © 1992 by Charlotte Raymond; 66 bottom and top, 67, and 167,
copyright © 1992 by Linda Zandler.

Library of Congress Cataloging-in-Publication Data
Linsley, Leslie.
Hooked rugs: an American folk art/by Leslie Linsley; photographs by Jon Aron.
Includes bibliographical references and index.
1. Rugs, Hooked—United States.   2. Folk art—United States.
I. Aron, Jon.   II. Title.
NK9112.L56   1991
746.7'4'0973—dc20   91-17100
CIP
ISBN 0-517-58102-7
1   3   5   7   9   10   8   6   4   2
First Edition

This book would not be the same without the help of so many people who were willing to give of their time, share their knowledge, make introductions on our behalf, and allow us into their homes to photograph their rugs.

I want to thank George Korn and Richard Kemble of Forager House Collection for their involvement in this project from its inception. Their extensive knowledge of folk art was invaluable, and their introduction to Barbara Johnson led to the inclusion of her exceptional rugs and the experience of a memorable interview.

Cathy Comins of Art Underfoot, Inc., graciously gave of her time to acquaint us with the work of contemporary rug hookers. Interior designer Beverly Ellsley worked with us in her home and showroom. Designer Trudy Dujardin allowed us to photograph the rugs in her historic home on Nantucket Island and in the homes of clients who had especially interesting rugs.

Collectors, consultants, dealers, restorers, and curators shared invaluable information that has greatly enriched this book. Others shared their rug collections and their hospitality while we photographed in their homes. Still others, living too far away to meet in person, took the trouble to send us their rugs. We are especially grateful to the following: Corrinne Burke, Howard Chadwick, Doug Copley of the New Hampshire Historic Society, Joan and David Curtis, Helaine and Burton Fendelman, Barbara Franco of the Minnesota Historic Society, Barbara Johnson, Ruth Johnston, Richard Kemble, Barbara and Peter Kenner, George Korn, Paula and William Laverty, Roslyn Logsdon, Barbara E. Merry, Polly Miller, Tish Murphy, Betty and Kenneth Olsen, Susan Parrish, Richardson Gallery, Julie Sanford, Avis Skinner, Jule Marie Smith, Grace and Elliott Snyder, Annette Stackpole, Marianne and Jon Swan, Rubens Teles, The Tiller Antiques, Lynn Traub of the De Cordova and Dana Museum in Lincoln, Massachusetts, Fran Willey, Jessica Woodle, and Mary Woodrum. And finally, for making introductions to friends with wonderful rugs, we want to thank Maddy Bohnsack, June and Henry Pfeiffer, and Liz Winship.

We especially want to thank Carol Southern at Clarkson Potter for the opportunity to do this book and for teaming us up with Pam Krauss, an intelligent and dedicated editor.

L. L. and J. A.

CONTENTS

PART I

An Introduction to Hooked Rugs
8

PART II

A Gallery of Hooked Rugs
22

PART III

Putting It Together
134

AN INTRODUCTION

TO HOOKED RUGS

THE HOOKED RUG, PAST AND PRESENT

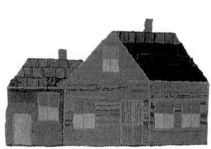

Rug hooking is one of a small handful of truly indigenous arts. A relatively recent innovation, the making of rugs by securing strips of cloth in a loosely woven base material first became popular in mid-nineteenth-century New England. Yet unlike quiltmaking, with which it shares a humble origin, rug hooking has only recently begun to attract the attention of collectors and curators. Today these graphic, often charmingly naive pieces are highly prized for their striking designs, craftsmanship, and social significance.

As with most home-grown crafts, rug hooking was born out of necessity coupled with a desire for creative expression. Just as early American homemakers pieced together scraps of fabrics both old and new to make patchwork quilts, strips cut from worn clothing were used to create hooked rugs. (In fact, New England rugs were often made with the same calico fabrics found in early quilts.) However, unlike quilts, which were subjected to repeated washing and which rarely survived hard use in good condition, sturdy hooked rugs often withstood constant use for a hundred years or more, passing from

Opposite: Studio of rug restorer Marianne Swan of Great Barrington, Massachusetts.

one generation to the next virtually unaltered.

While rural women originally made rugs to cover bare floors, later rug hookers often created pieces specifically in order to sell them. Many, especially those living in poor or isolated communities, formed cottage industries for this purpose, exporting their finished pieces to more affluent, urban areas. This brought income to families during lean winter months and served to relieve boredom as well. This profitable outlet for hooked rugs led to even greater popularity for the craft.

During the Depression, rug hooking came into its own as a diversion or leisure-time activity. Experts and teachers formed classes to teach the rudiments of rug hooking and women took up the craft as a means of personal expression rather than as a source of income or out of necessity. By the 1940s, rug hooking was well established as a hobby, and classes became a popular pastime for many women. Today, contemporary fiber artisans find an enthusiastic audience for their work, and classes for those interested in learning rug hooking as a hobby are burgeoning.

Recently, shows devoted entirely to early hooked rugs as well as contemporary works in this medium have been sponsored by such prestigious organizations as the Textile Museum in Washington, D.C., the Squibb Corporation in their New Jersey gallery, the Museum of American Folk Art and the American Craft Museum in New York City, as well as by many others throughout the country. Discriminating appreciators of folk art have made hooked rugs among the most desirable of all collectibles. Today one sees more hooked rugs than ever before included in the catalogs of respected auction houses, and antiques dealers have placed a great value on the hooked rugs they own. This humble art has indeed come a long way.

Influences on the Evolution of Rug Hooking

The genesis of rug hooking can be traced to 1840 and the eastern seaboard, and the craft has changed little since that time. Rug hooking is a rather simple process in which loops of wool or cotton fabric are secured in an even-weave background to create a pattern or illustration. In general the designs were drawn from scenes of everyday life: animals, flowers, children at play, or whatever the designer most cherished. The earliest rug hookers were uninhibited when it came to drawing their subjects, evidenced by a lack of concern for accuracy of scale and perspective; animals are often distorted and flowers frequently dwarf houses in the same scene. After the introduction of stamped patterns in 1850, fewer original illustrations were created, and those early rugs are the most sought after for their charming, primitive quality and whimsical subjects.

When patternmakers began selling prestenciled patterns on burlap, designs became more formal and stiff. Rugs made after 1875 were generally made from kits that indicated color placements as well as the designs, further contributing to the uniformity of later rugs. Prestenciled color-printed patterns became so popular they all but replaced original designs that could be identified by their regional differences and primitive whimsy. Yet even then, some free spirits merely used the rug patterns as a point of departure, rendering them in their own style and colors. It is often amusing to trace the origin of a particular rug design and compare the individual's interpretation to the original execution.

Perhaps the first to package and market hooked rug patterns was Edward Sands Frost, a tin peddler from Maine whose wife was a rug maker. At her suggestion, Frost designed metal stencil patterns that he applied to burlap. He began taking them on his route in 1868, and within eight years had an inventory of 180 different rug designs. These patterns enabled women with little or no drawing ability to execute perfectly designed rugs. Rugs made from a Frost pattern are especially easy to identify; their designs are overly symmetrical and the animals and flowers are stiff. However, his simplified patterns made rug hooking accessible to an eager new audience, and by the end of the nineteenth century the craft was no longer confined to New England and the Atlantic seacoast, but had spread throughout the United States and into England. Between 1868 and 1900, thousands of rugs were made from printed patterns.

Decorating magazines of the time popularized the craft by showing rugs in appealing room settings. Homer Eaton Keyes, editor of *Antiques* magazine in the 1920s, was particularly interested in the origin of hooked rugs and published a number of articles on the subject, furthering the interest of collectors and dealers.

In the 1930s, rug hooking was a popular avocation. Women gathered in small, informal groups, reminiscent of quilting bees, for a few hours of rug hooking. From these small, informal get-togethers, more organized workshops and classes developed. One teacher, Caroline Saunders, influenced many students, some of whom became noted designers and teachers. The best known were Pearl McGown, Louise Hunter Zeiser, and Edith Dana, who would become major influences on the future designs of hooked rugs. Louise Zeiser is responsible for preserving many antique and original designs in the form of patterns, which are still available.

A Burgeoning Cottage Industry

By the early twentieth century, commercial rug hooking had developed into a cottage industry throughout the eastern United States and Canada as well. Perhaps the best-known rug hooking collective was the Grenfell Mission in Newfoundland. There was little relief in Labrador from the long, bleak winters, and local subsistence depended mainly on fishing and fur trapping. Rug hooking, however, was already a popular pastime with local residents when Dr. Wilfred Grenfell arrived on a hospital ship in 1890. Recognizing the potential market for these distinctive pieces, he organized the local artisans into a formal collective, and the unusual rugs produced by the Mission became renowned for their cool, pale tones and tightly woven textures. Today these rugs are prized collectibles and even without a label are easily identified by their colors and naturalistic subject matter.

By the end of the nineteenth century, the increased availability and accessible prices of manufactured goods sent handcrafts into decline. Inexpensive carpeting was readily available and rug hooking was all but a lost art, kept alive only by a small group of designers dedicated to preserving the tradition of American craftsmanship. These same individuals formed the core of the Arts and Crafts Movement.

One such designer was Mrs. Helen R. Albee, a New Hampshire woman, who established a home industry at the start of the 1900s with the goals of introducing better designs and providing a source of income to local farm women. Rug hooking had never fallen from favor in the less affluent areas, and most farmhouses in the region were filled with rugs. But these tended to be crudely designed and made of fabrics so worn and threadbare that they were suitable for only the most modest uses.

Mrs. Albee helped the artisans to upgrade both their materials and their designs, experimenting with fabrics to achieve a desirable pile and texture. She tried different dyeing techniques until she was able to produce the subtle, soft colors she wanted for her designs. Of her strong, simple designs Mrs. Albee said, "The decorative forms used by the Indians, as by all primitive peoples, appealed to me greatly, yet their symbolism would be meaningless to us, however expressive of Indian religion and legendary lore. The only thing to do was to think myself back to the viewpoint of the primitive craftsman and then let the designs grow of themselves from the clear and simple thought out to inevitable combinations of form and color."

Ultimately, the rugs made in the Pequaket, New Hampshire, area under Mrs. Albee's direction were considered the most beautiful of their time. Her success led to the establishment of similar cottage industries intended primarily to further the Arts and Crafts Movement while generating income for remote regions. Indeed, many communities from Maine to North Carolina were producing rugs at the time. Well known among these were the Cranberry Isle Industry of Maine, sponsored by Amy Mali Hicks, and the Subbekashe Rug Industry in Belchertown, Massachusetts, started in 1902 by Lucy D. Thomson, whose group produced rugs that recalled American Indian motifs, much like the designs created by Helen Albee. Community groups also formed in Virginia, Kentucky, and Tennessee between 1918 and the 1930s to promote hooked rugs; the women sold their rugs from their homes, at roadside stands, or through an organization that would ship them off to fashionable city stores.

The vision of those first entrepreneurs was realized in a relatively short span of time. Not only did hundreds of households benefit from a newly created home business, but the industry furthered a keener awareness of native handcrafts.

Dating

Dating and cataloging hooked rugs is a favorite pastime of collectors, art historians, and dealers. It can, however, be a frustrating task since so few of them are documented. "One reason it's often difficult to date these rugs," says Barbara Franco, an art historian, "is that many people confuse them with the needlework and yarn-sewn rugs that were made in the late eighteenth and early nineteenth centuries." Even when a date is worked into the design, it doesn't necessarily reflect when the rug was made, because important events, such as a wedding or birthday, were often commemorated in hooked rugs. Unlike quilts, which were signed and dated by the quiltmaker upon completion, rugs can be considerably younger than suggested by any dates worked into the pieces.

Color is one of the clues collectors and historians use to determine the provenance of hooked rugs, but it is at best an imperfect indicator. Fabric technology was changing rapidly in the nineteenth century and these changes are reflected in the materials used in rug hooking. Early-nineteenth-century rugs are generally faded because the vegetable dyes used in manufactured fabric were not colorfast. However, rugs that were stored carefully often remain quite vivid and bright. The advent of synthetic dyes at the end of the nineteenth century adds further to the confusion; while these dyes were intended to be colorfast and should, therefore, remain vividly colored, they weren't yet perfected and some of the rugs made with the new, bright colors of this period appear as muted and faded as much older rugs.

The background material may also afford some clues to a rug's age. The earliest rugs were made on a foundation of linen or hemp. However, once burlap was introduced, it almost entirely replaced linen or hemp as a rug backing because it was so well suited to this craft. The coarse fabric, used to wrap raw goods and for grain and feed sacks, was readily available and allowed the fabric strips to be pulled through with a crochet or button hook more easily than did the closely woven linen. And when opened at the seams, a feed or flour sack was the perfect size for a hearth rug. Therefore, rugs hooked on burlap are generally presumed to date after 1850, and those made on linen are almost always from an earlier period.

Aside from these few indicators for dating rugs, it is amazing how little information we have to substantiate the history of this textile art. Scanty or incorrect documentation, misinformation, and contradictions have made it difficult for museum curators, collectors, and art historians to document hooked rugs accurately. Fortunately we are beginning to recognize the importance of preservation and have been able to foster more awareness of our rich heritage in the decorative arts.

Contemporary Interest

Today we are once again experiencing a resurgence of interest in the folk craft of rug hooking, part of a larger revival in all forms of handcrafts. As in quilting, some rug hookers are interested in re-creating and keeping alive the old patterns as part of an ongoing tradition. These artisans are dedicated to using original techniques to create authentic reproductions of early designs.

Other crafters are experimenting with modern interpretations and combining old techniques with new textures and patterns, which has resulted in some interesting rugs of contemporary design. Perhaps the thoughts expressed by Helen Albee, an early-twentieth-century designer, represent the attitude that has always inspired folk artists in creative endeavors: "The work itself is sufficient evidence that the process opens up vistas of inquiry about design, the use of materials and colors, and the pleasure felt from doing work that is an outgrowth of the imagination."

Today many of these new pieces are bought and collected as creative works of art. Cathy Comins, the founder and president of Art Underfoot, Inc., is an enterprising woman interested in hooked rugs as both an art and a craft. Much like the Craft Guilds of the 1930s and 1940s, her company brings together rug hookers and hooked rug appreciators, and today represents more than a hundred folk and fine-fiber artists from California to Maine. The collection that she's assembled features original designs, rugs reproduced from traditional patterns, and rugs custom-made for specific decorating needs. Hers is a unique service designed to further the awareness of rug hooking as an art while providing an outlet for contemporary crafters to derive an income from their craft.

Historically, rug hooking has always responded to the prevailing economic and cultural climate. It has provided a means of income in lean times, a pleasant diversion during a depression, a leisure-time activity for periods of prosperity, and now a medium for contemporary craftworkers. It is no wonder that early hooked rugs have taken a valued place among the American folk arts. In the last decade, we have begun to appreciate hooked rugs for their design, craftsmanship, and historic value. This appreciation will enable us to continue to learn more about hooked rugs and their contributions in documenting the evolution of the decorative arts in this country.

HOW TO HOOK A RUG: MATERIALS AND TECHNIQUES

Most rug hookers will tell you that anyone can make a hooked rug. The materials are few and the tools simple. All you need are a piece of burlap or monk's cloth with a design marked on it, a rug hook, and narrow strips of wool fabric in the desired colors. Some crafters like to work with the material on either a lap frame or one that stands on the floor. Burlap is stiffer than even-weave monk's cloth and is therefore easier to work on your lap without a frame. The monk's cloth is softer and more pliable and is best worked when mounted over a frame.

The technique is simple. First the wool is cut into strips either by hand with long fabric sheers or by a cutting device made specifically for this purpose. Next a design is drawn on the foundation material. The strips of wool are then pulled up through the mesh of the background fabric with a small hook, much like a crochet hook with a wooden handle, to form a pile.

Opposite: Detail of Pennsylvania Horse (page 131)

The choice of colors and textures is what brings subtlety and depth to hooked pieces. Like many of the new breed of creative rug hookers, Polly Miller, of Nantucket, Massachusetts, cuts her strips from worn-out wool clothing just as the early hookers did. However, she feels that it's also acceptable to mix in new remnants, as it's not always easy to find a diverse range of colors from worn clothing alone. By mixing old and new, different shadings can be achieved in the rugs. Further, the combination of different weights and thicknesses of wool will bring a richness, an interesting variety of textures and colors, to a rug design. It is not advisable, however, to mix different fibers; when synthetics and wools are used together, for example, the abrasion of the strips against one another can cause the less-sturdy wool to wear out faster. This creates an unappealing unevenness that can shorten the rug's life.

Much of the richness in a hooked rug comes from the creative use of different shades of color. If you don't have the precise colors you want for your design, it's not difficult to dye your own. For some, experimenting with dyes to create unique colors is an exciting part of the process.

Contemporary folk artist Jule Marie Smith from Ballston Spa, New York, sums up the feeling of many rug designers when she says, "Building the colors in a rug is a very complex and time-consuming task, but is also very rewarding, especially when you successfully achieve a certain subtlety."

Creating a Design

Before you can hook a rug, you'll need a pattern. Until a few years ago, original work was not encouraged in this particular craft. Those who set up workshops and established teaching methods believed that the old patterns and traditional methods of hand dyeing should be used exclusively. With the formation of the Association of Traditional Hooking Arts (ATHA), interested crafters attended various rug symposia where they immersed themselves in the world of color and design, examining the possibilities of the medium. We are now seeing the results of their explorations in more original and exciting new designs.

While there are many prestenciled patterns available, designing your own can be challenging and rewarding. You might also combine design elements taken from a variety of sources, including old rugs. Most of Polly Miller's rugs are original, but sometimes she enjoys reproducing a design that attracts her. She often takes liberties with them, sometimes using brighter colors, knowing they'll fade with wear. She might, for example, in order to frame the illustration, add a dark border around a rug that she's reproducing.

If you are creating your own design, it can be drawn freehand on the burlap or monk's cloth. If you are transferring an existing pattern (see pages 144 to 162), place a piece of clear plastic over the design and trace it with a felt-tip marker. Next, pin the foundation material over the plastic drawing and tape this to a sheet of glass. Place a bright light under the glass so you can see the design through the foundation and trace the design onto the material. It may be necessary to trace the design in sections if the rug is very large. If you don't find it cumbersome, you might tape the design and fabric to a window and use the natural light to trace the design onto the fabric.

Once the design has been transferred to the

background, it is advisable to run a line of matching stitching approximately an inch beyond the design all around to prevent fraying while the piece is worked. It can then be worked either on your lap or stretched on a frame. A frame holds the work taut and allows you to use both hands freely. If the piece is small, the fabric can be mounted on an artist's stretcher or a small lap frame. A large embroidery hoop can also serve as a frame. They are inexpensive and readily available in fabric or yarn shops.

Cutting the Wool

Begin by cutting your wool into strips approximately ¼ inch wide and short enough to work with comfortably, perhaps 12 to 18 inches long. A small hand-operated cutting machine that mounts onto the edge of a table makes it possible to cut the wool into uniform narrow strips approximately ⅛ to ¼ inch wide. The machine is not absolutely necessary since the strips can be cut by hand, but

Wool is cut into narrow strips by means of a portable stripper.

it does make this step much easier and quicker. To estimate the amount of wool needed in each color, it is necessary to hook a small area with the weight and texture that will be used. This will not be absolutely accurate, as hooking varies within a design, but it will enable you to approximate the number of strips needed. Keep in mind that the background will be completed last and should be worked in a color that will enhance the design and show it off to best advantage. Sometimes a soft tweed works well, providing both a pale color and some texture.

Hooking the Design

Once you have a good supply of fabric strips in a range of colors, you can begin working the design. Start with the central motifs or image. Hold the handle of the hook comfortably in your hand. With the other hand, hold a strip of wool beneath the pattern. Insert the hook through the top of the foundation, hook the wool strip, and pull the short end up through the top. Always pull the ends to the top rather than leaving them underneath; as you finish a section, the ends can be cut even with the loops.

Next, insert the hook into an adjacent hole in the foundation fabric and pull up a loop of fabric. Keep the strip on the hook as you pull down from the underside to create a loop about ⅛ inch high. After you do this several times you'll develop a rhythm and the loops will be fairly even. The loops should be comfortably touching. You don't have to work every hole in your mesh, but the closer together you place the loops, the tighter the weave. If they are too far apart, the rug will be weak, because it's the pressure of one loop against

Top: A Chinese Hexagonal design is drawn on monk's cloth, then attached to a frame for hooking.

Above: The ends of the wool are cut even with the top loops after each section is completed.

Left: Contemporary rug hooker Polly Miller is working on an original design in her Nantucket Island studio.

another that holds everything together. When you reach the end of the strip, once again pull the loose end to the front of the piece. The underside of the foundation should be smooth to the touch. There is no need to tie off anything in rug hooking.

Although it is easiest to work across the piece in rows, experienced rug makers generally work in a staggered fashion rather than lining the loops up in exactly the same direction. As you work along a row, for example, you skip over a square, or work one square in the row below every so often to add strength as well as interest. The skipped squares can be worked later from another direction. By varying the direction in which you work, it is possible to change the look of a design. If, for example, you are hooking a green hill, by changing the direction of the loop placement you can create dimension.

From time to time check the design on the underside of the piece; it isn't always clear from the top. The underside will give you an idea of what the pattern will look like after the rug has been used and the loops are flattened. Be sure to pull all ends to the top and clip evenly.

Hooking the Background

Once the designs are hooked, you will fill in the background area. It is a good idea to fill in the area around the design elements first. Then you can hook either across in straight lines or in a random pattern to create interest and shading. You can even hook the background in patterns, like swirls or leaf shapes. This is especially useful if you run out of your wool and have to work with another weight or a slightly different color. Different wools will never match exactly, unless you've dyed the wool yourself. But this slight difference can add depth and variety to your design.

Binding

The edges of a rug are the most vulnerable because they receive the greatest amount of wear. This is why most rugs are edged with a binding. Binding tape comes in rolls of 1¼-inch-wide twill. It can match the background or a color in the design, or you might want to use a dark binding to hide the eventual dirt and wear it will receive.

Use heavy-duty thread to slipstitch binding tape all around the front of the finished rug as close to the last row of loops as possible. Cut off the excess foundation fabric up to the stitched line and miter the corners. Fold the tape and fabric back approximately ½ inch beyond the last row of hooking and hem.

Blocking

If your rug is too large to fit on an ironing board, pad a table or the floor with several layers of toweling. Place the finished rug face down on the towels and steam-press from the wrong side. This will enable you to block the rug and adjust any distortions or curling at the edges.

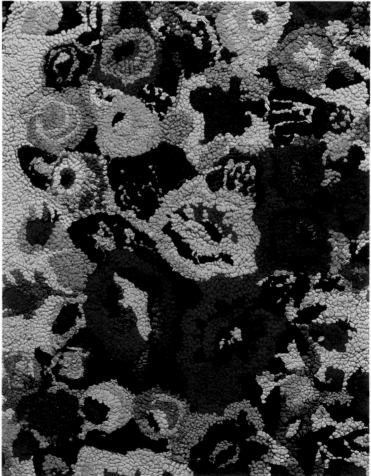

Above right: Young Riders (see page 89) is bound in a pale twill that complements the background shade. The colors have softened with many years of constant use.

Right: Detail of the controlled hooking technique and the rug maker's excellent ability to create depth with shading. This Country Garden rug (see page 94) does not appear to have been used extensively.

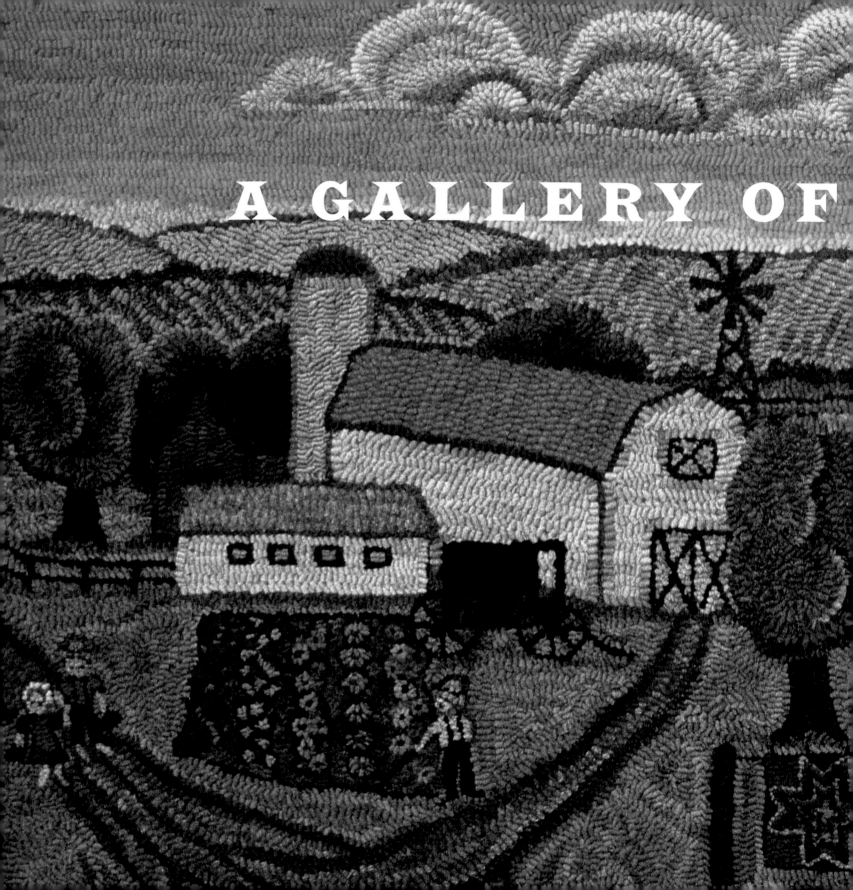

A GALLERY OF

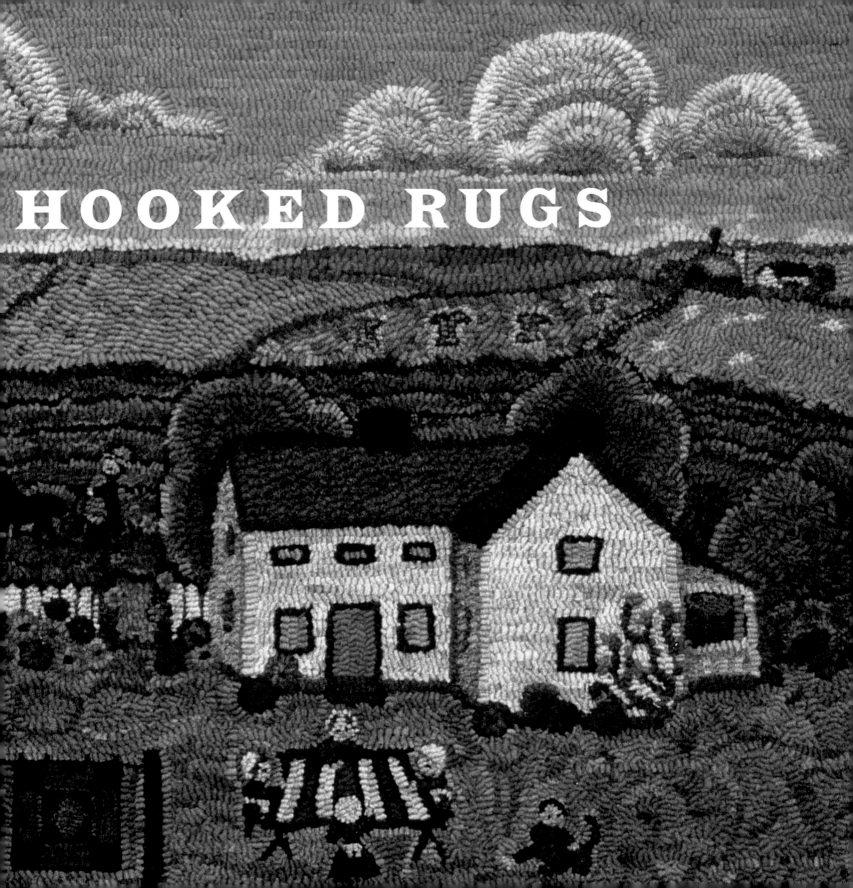

HOOKED RUGS

GEOMETRIC AND ABSTRACT DESIGNS

Many early rug hookers favored geometric patterns for using up scraps of multicolored wools. Geometric designs were also well suited to beginning rug makers, who found the straight lines and regular patterns easy to master. Patchwork quilt patterns were readily adapted for rug making and this influence is apparent in early as well as contemporary rugs.

Common graphic symbols—such as hearts, stars, moons, and crosses— were often incorporated into a design. They were often used to create a border, and sometimes even dominated the entire rug.

Abstract designs were also popular and often reflected the period in which they were made. Art Deco and Oriental patterns in hooked rugs of the nineteenth century offered an inexpensive alternative to authentic Oriental and manufactured rugs.

LIBERTY CAP
Above: *Made of cotton and wool on burlap, this rug was made in Frederick, Maryland, in 1895 and was part of the Frederick Hanson Collection. 46½″ × 26½″*

CHINESE HEXAGON
Opposite: *Polly Miller designed and made this 3′ × 5′ rug for the Nantucket Looms.*

RUGS
INSPIRED BY
QUILTS

It is fair to assume that early rug makers also made quilts. The patterns were familiar to them and they were easily adaptable. It was not uncommon to find a Log Cabin quilt on the bed and a Log Cabin hooked rug on the floor. This popular quilt design could be made to fit any size rug, from a runner to a piece large enough to fill a room.

Block patterns were the most effective of all geometric designs. Sometimes known as the Carpet pattern, a row of arranged squares forming a design could be used to cover a large area. It was a simple matter to cut a template from a piece of cardboard and move it over the burlap in order to draw the lines.

Diamonds were also popular, affording an opportunity to use different color combinations. The Double Wedding Ring was another favorite.

FOLK ART ALBUM QUILT PATTERN
The 36″ × 58″ rug dominating this entryway is a bold interpretation of a Zeiser Album Quilt pattern in the home of artist Richard Kemble and folk art dealer George Korn. It adds excitement and vibrant colors to the environment.
On the table a ceramic bowl by well-known artisan Hannelore Fasciszewski is filled with rare blown-glass "witches' balls." A "hit-or-miss" rug, made of colorful leftovers, is used inside the doorway.

Sometimes referred to as a China Plate pattern or a Saucer pattern, this was first popular with quilt-makers at the time of the Civil War, and came into vogue again in the 1920s and 1930s. It was an easy pattern to create because it could be made by moving a saucer or dinner plate about the rug in order to draw the pattern. Any simple device like this for creating a pattern appealed to rug makers.

Some rugs combined geometrics with figurative or floral designs, just as appliquéd quilts did. Patterns such as the Album Quilt were originally drawn by rug-hooking teachers such as Caroline

Saunders and Louise Hunter Zeiser, who designed and drew patterns for hundreds of rugs. Her son Robert H. Zeiser has for many years made these patterns available for rug hookers. (See Rug-Hooking Supplies, page 165).

The Cathedral Window is a repeat pattern that was originally done in one color scheme. Vera Bisbee Underhill, a rug maker, teacher, and author in the late 1940s and early 1950s, emphasized the idea of using one color combination to avoid "the appearance of a number of Cathedral Windows that have somehow melted and run together."

TUMBLING BLOCKS AND CATHEDRAL PATTERN
Two simple geometric rugs, made in the mid-twentieth century, work well in the same room. One is made of curves designed with subtle colors; the other is bold with straight lines. The dominant rug is an interpretation of the Tumbling Blocks quilt pattern. Here a black border and a gray center set off the light and dark shades of bright colors used on the blocks. The needlepoint pillows, "Quiet Forest," are by artist Richard Kemble and the New England candlestand holds Nantucket lightship baskets, an early sea-related craft. Tumbling Blocks 30″ × 52″; Cathedral Pattern 24″ × 36″

FALLING CARDS
The subtle colors and expert craftsmanship make this early-twentieth-century rug a key element in a carefully decorated room. Its colors are echoed in the appliqué quilt wallhanging, patchwork pillows, painted blanket chest, and upholstered furniture. The architectural details of the Federal-style molding around the windows are painted a subtle Shaker green. The combination of painted furniture and country accessories used sparingly makes this room a classic in the American folk art tradition. 4′ × 6½′

QUILT PATTERNS

Squares of a Log Cabin motif alternate with Cathedral Windows rendered in a rainbow of nonrepeating colors. The result is an unusual 12' × 14' rug of vibrant colors that the current owner bought in Maine.

The early one-patch quilt and miniature patchwork pillows on the bed make this an inviting guest bedroom. Antique lace and embroidered pillowcases are light and delicate against the dark wood of the headboard. The bed and dresser are part of a complete cottage set. While these pieces were manufactured, each was individually painted with scenes or floral designs.

DOUBLE WEDDING RING

This 36" × 38" rug made in the 1920s could have been part of a bride's hope chest. The placement of the rug on top of a Persian carpet shows how versatile hooked rugs can be. Similar colors in both rugs must have been obvious to Kemble and Korn when they chose to combine these two elements in the room.

LOG CABIN

In this rug, made in 1940 by Annette Stackpole, the alternating red and blue centers of each square are consistent and scraps of different colors were used to fill the surrounding areas. 28" × 38"

GRAPHIC SYMBOLS

Graphic symbols appear frequently in hooked rugs. Often they were used as part of a larger theme, like in the Red Star rug (page 42), which is bordered by stars and hearts. But in many cases, graphic symbols themselves served as the rug's primary image. The significance of these symbols may have changed over the years, but their visual impact remains strong.

Contemporary rug hooker Tish Murphy intends the underlying feel of her rugs to be "contemporary folk." Many of the symbols and subjects she uses—hearts, stars, and domestic animals— appear repeatedly in historic examples. Ms. Murphy puts these familiar motifs in a contemporary context, sometimes with reference to nineteenth- and twentieth-century decorative and graphic arts.

CASSIOPEIA
Sailors' use of stars in hooked rugs continues in this design by rug hooker/sailor Polly Miller. She says, "The constellation Cassiopeia is a friendly sight, visible while sailing in southern waters." The center motif portrays the constellation, which Polly says is like a friend in the sky when she's sailing up from the Caribbean. This 32" × 38" rug was made in 1989 on Nantucket Island. The border is based on a nineteenth-century rug in Barbara Johnson's collection. Ms. Johnson calls her rug "Eight-Star Prize."

"HEART OF IT ALL"
This rug by Tish Murphy is a blending of symbol and context. The design for this rug evolved through a series of events. Tish had been hooking a number of small hearts to use as color samples. Separately, she had been making thumbnail sketches of flag motifs, captivated by the graphic force of stars and stripes. She says, "When controversy over the flag-burning issue arose, the two images fused in my mind. It was a happy union of visual and emotional impact." Traditional hooking with hand-dyed wool on monk's cloth backing, 1989. 31" square

MALTESE CROSS PATTERN
This pattern is typical of rugs made in the mid-1800s, and demonstrates how a basic pattern of squares can be interpreted in an interesting way. The use of colors reflects an artistic sense of style and tells us much about the rug maker. A more common way to hook this pattern would have been to use up scraps of colorful wool. Many creative craftworkers took basic patterns such as this and, by their choice of colors, made them into beautiful rugs. 24" × 38". A scale pattern for this rug appears on pages 146 to 147.

SIX-POINTED STAR

Left: *This rug might have been made by a young sailor during long, inactive times aboard ship. The bold red star surrounded by full and half moons, clovers, and a fish are symbols frequently used by sailors, and the combination creates a picture that portends good luck at sea.*

The owner, Susan Parrish, is a dealer in American Indian art who has decorated her home in the southwestern tradition. The rug, which was made in 1923 and is 36" square, was a recent find and one that seems to have been made for this room.

HEART, HOME, AND CROSS

Right: *The only information we have about this early rug is that it was made by a patient in a psychiatric institution. Its very lack of formality gives this rug its energy. The heart, the cross, and the house are common folk art images, often found in primitive rugs. Here, they are presented in a direct and uncontrived way, expressing basic values.*

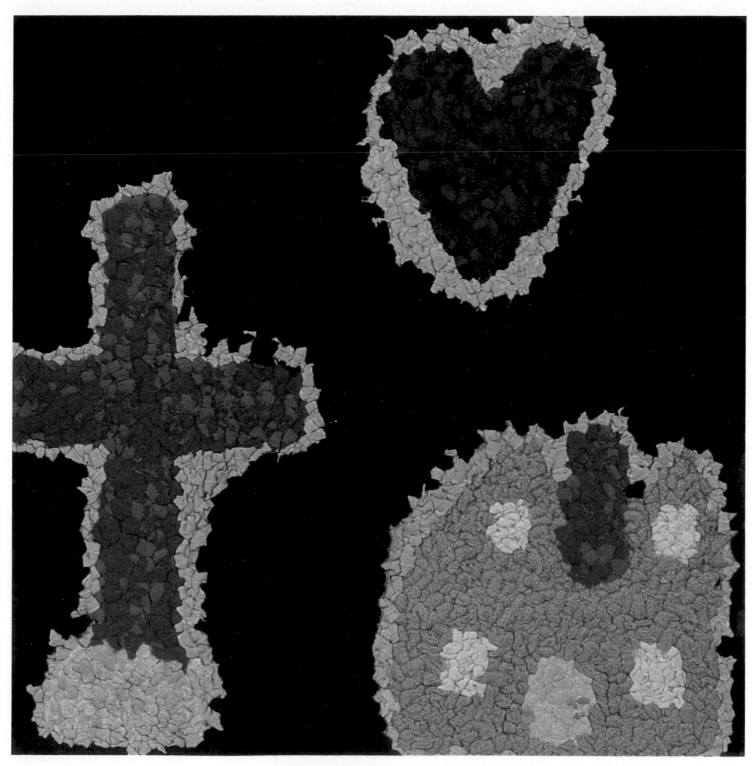

A Gallery of Hooked Rugs

37

HIT-OR-MISS BACKGROUNDS

Hit-or-miss backgrounds are the most common texture in hooked rugs. After making several rugs, the early crafters would gather the scraps and hook them back and forth across a rug, choosing colors haphazardly for a textural rather than graphic effect. This is the easiest and most uninhibited form of hooking.

Sometimes, however, hooking back and forth in this manner could be become rather tedious, and it is not unusual to see a small geometric design introduced to break up the background, adding interest for both the artisan and the viewer.

Although early rug hookers tended to fill their backgrounds in a random and offhanded way, as the art evolved, the importance of the background to a piece's overall effect earned careful consideration. Fran Willey, a contemporary rug maker, gives special attention to the backgrounds of her rugs; her objective is to allow colors to play off one another rather than to cause one to steal the show (see pages 50 and 51).

WARM FRIENDSHIP
Dated 1920, this 45½" × 78½" rug was found in Mohawk, New York. It was made of rayon knits on burlap and is part of Barbara Johnson's collection. This early rug maker obviously worked this rug without regard to conventional measuring techniques. It is a creative use of leftover material in a kaleidoscopic pattern, naively rendered.

Deco Borders

Left: *An Art Deco border graces this matched set of hit-or-miss rugs. The black border serves as a frame around each one. While these scrap bag–type rugs are not considered particularly valuable by most rug dealers, they are still prized by collectors for their charm. It's unusual to find a matched pair such as these two. Shown here in the country bedroom of an 1800 house, these rugs measuring 23″ × 62″ would fit into a contemporary setting as well.*

Game Board

Right: *Interior designer Beverly Ellsley found a creative way to display a small square rug. On her kitchen farm table, the subdued colors of barn red and Shaker blue are set off by a background of cream and borders of black. The rug picks up the colors of the tapestry in the chairs and seems right at home in this Connecticut log cabin house. Approximately 32″ square*

ABSTRACT DESIGNS

Regular geometric forms are only one aspect of abstract rug designs. From the beginning, rug hookers designed rugs with random striations, shapes, and lines in every imaginable color and configuration. Since they predated Picasso, Braque, Kandinsky, and Mondrian by a century or more, contemporary notions of abstract art didn't figure into these creations.

In most cases, early rug makers designed abstract rugs simply to use up scrap wool that would otherwise have gone to waste. Yet these rugs are not simply leftovers. Some betray a keen sense of color.

RED STAR

Reminiscent of a contemporary abstract painting, this early 30″ × 48″ cotton and wool rug combines bold graphic shapes of stars, hearts, squares, and rectangles. It was found in Maine and now hangs over a marble fireplace in the dining room of a Federal-style brownstone in New York. While this is a wonderful example of late-nineteenth-century folk art, one can just as easily imagine it hanging in a contemporary environment as an example of modern art.

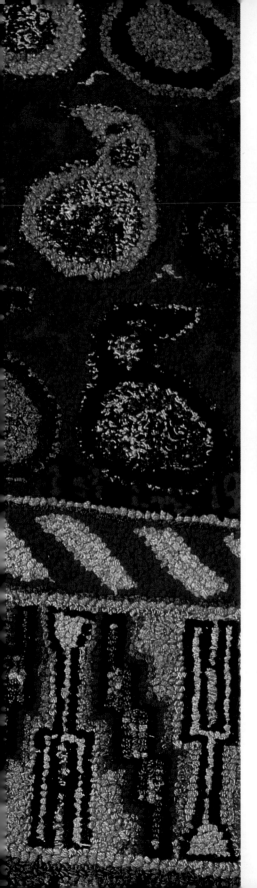

PAISLEY
Left and above: *The owner of this rug, signed, "From Marian, Harold and Rowe Austin on June 15 in 1941," assures us that it is a paisley design, even though one might guess that the rug maker had penguins in mind when creating it. The effect of the overall pattern and borders is that of an Oriental carpet. It is a rare and unusual rug and fits perfectly in this comfortable country den. The crazy quilt on the wall was made with remnants of velvet and satin. Interesting appliquéd figures and symbols are interspersed throughout. The eclectic mix of accessories—Chinese lamp, dough trough coffee table, Indian and embroidered pillows —demonstrates the owner's sense of style. Made in 1941, the rug measures 9' × 9'.*

REFLECTIONS IN
RED AND BLUE
Following spread: *Flowing curves and subtle colors of red, blue, gray, and beige outlined in black create a graceful abstract design. Made in 1910, the rug measures 31" × 48" and was found in Indiana.*

MONDRIAN

Opposite: Antique quilts, painted furniture, and American Indian art surround this Art Deco rug in Susan Parrish's antiques shop in New York City. A striking nonobjective composition, this rug owes much to artists like Piet Mondrian. 48″ × 74″

The small farm scene is rendered in outline and filled in with solid, flat colors that create a posterlike feeling. The hooking was done in horizontal rows throughout, emphasizing surface texture. 19″ × 31″

BOSTON PAVEMENT

Placing this rug at the bottom of a stairway makes a dramatic impact. Reminiscent of mosaic tile work, the tiny squares combine to make a bright, vibrating pattern when viewed close up and a bold, graphic pattern from a distance.

It is easy to see the inspiration for this rug, which may indeed have originated in Boston, Massachusetts. The owner, Betty Olsen, finds most of her rugs at flea markets, yard sales, and open-air antiques fairs all over the Northeast, and has no details regarding its original date. 34″ × 53″

PIANO RUG

It was common practice to place a small Oriental rug beneath the pedals of a piano, for both decorative and practical reasons. Here a hooked rug takes the place of a more formal floor cover. The black grand piano stands in contrast to the contemporary bench made by furniture designer George Takashima. The 24″ × 36″ rug is quite elegant in this environment.

RED AND GRAY
WALLHANGING
*In this abstract composition,
artist Fran Willey
experimented with three
different red dyes to create the
tints and shades in the main
motif. The subtle background
is made up of many different
shades of gray.*

COMPOSITION IN BLACK
Departures from traditional rug hooking techniques are noticeable in this piece by Fran Willey, which features a solid black background, plastic fibers, and reflective threads.

PEOPLE, PLACES, AND THINGS

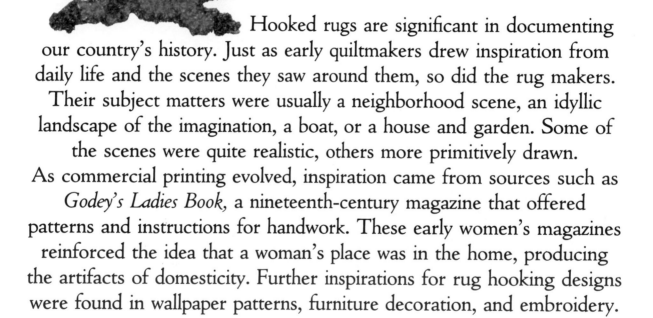

Hooked rugs are significant in documenting our country's history. Just as early quiltmakers drew inspiration from daily life and the scenes they saw around them, so did the rug makers. Their subject matters were usually a neighborhood scene, an idyllic landscape of the imagination, a boat, or a house and garden. Some of the scenes were quite realistic, others more primitively drawn. As commercial printing evolved, inspiration came from sources such as *Godey's Ladies Book,* a nineteenth-century magazine that offered patterns and instructions for handwork. These early women's magazines reinforced the idea that a woman's place was in the home, producing the artifacts of domesticity. Further inspirations for rug hooking designs were found in wallpaper patterns, furniture decoration, and embroidery.

FOX HUNT
Detail of Fox Hunt by Jule Marie Smith. The rug can be seen in its entirety on page 58.

PICTORIALS

Figurative rugs made a hundred years ago reveal much about the rug makers and how they lived. The same is true today. Some crafters and artists use the medium of hooked rugs to express highly personal views or images.

Folk artists like Maine rug maker Barbara Merry create rugs that have the same "primitive" quality that attracts us to early rugs. Ms. Merry's rugs record bits and pieces of her rural past as well as family events and community scenes in her country life today. The illustration is often reminiscent of things we associate with the past. Indeed, several of Ms. Merry's rugs caused quite a stir when, unbeknownst to her, an antiques dealer passed off her rugs as early folk art. The story is an example of how difficult it can be to date rugs.

For twenty-four years, Barbara Merry enjoyed rug making as a hobby, giving away most of her creations to friends and relatives. When her hus-

ADAM AND EVE
Dated 1910, this rug was made in New Jersey of rayon on burlap. The maker's initials, D. F. S., are hooked into the bottom center of the rug, which is 22½" × 29" and is part of Barbara Johnson's collection.

band became ill, she began to sell the rugs to bring in extra income. This change, from hobbyist to professional, inadvertently made her a national folk hero when a shrewd dealer saw the rugs and bought all he could get his hands on. The dealer then advertised the rugs in the *Maine Antiques Digest,* claiming they had been made by Barbara Merry, a woman who had died in 1910.

Several factors contributed to making the rugs seem authentically primitive: Merry's use of early materials, her subject matter, and the fact that she signs her full name or initials. Word of this legendary twentieth-century rug hooker, who had made only four or five rugs before her death, was circulated and the rugs were purchased by collectors as well as the Baltimore Museum. Textile consultants and museum curators authenticated the rugs as antiques. Ms. Merry was completely unaware that the rugs she had been selling for under fifty dollars were now sought after by collectors for twenty times that amount.

The story has a happy ending. Despite the hoax, or perhaps because of the publicity it brought, Barbara Merry now has a constant backlog of orders. Her work has gained a wider audience of people who might not otherwise have discovered this contemporary folk artist.

PLANTATION WASHERWOMAN
Barbara Merry shares a bit of her life in each of her rugs. "I try to capture a quiet way of life," she says. Pieced into the rugs are scenes that she remembers from her mother's family on Sears Island, where they lived in 1915. This rug measures 34½" × 47".

ROCKLAND, MAINE, FISH MARKET

This is a fine example of a rug by contemporary folk artist Barbara Merry of Thorndike, Maine, whose designs incorporate many aspects of coastal Maine, where she grew up. Her aesthetic sense and keen memory help her to visualize a scene before drawing it on the burlap background. In this rug, owned by Ms. Merry's stepnephew, Leslie Merry, the fish market is seen on the left and the fish processing plant on the right.

FOX HUNT
This 3' × 5' rug was made in 1988 by Jule Marie Smith. Her interest in fox hunting was piqued by English prints of hunts. The scene is set in late autumn and the wools were dyed to suggest the season's many tones of reds and browns.

HOME SWEET HOME
A primitive example of a welcome mat with a hit-or-miss background. Approximately 26" × 34".

HOUSE WITH PATH

Left: *This simple house drawing could have been designed for a child's room. The playful border is made up of boldly colored blocks with triangles in each corner. The coloring-book quality of solid colors heavily outlined in black was not common in hooked rugs. Made of wool on burlap, this rug is 24″ × 39″. A scale pattern for it appears on page 162.*

RED AND BLUE HOUSE

Right: *It is unusual to find an illustration of a house that doesn't place it squarely in the center of the rug. This house is placed off-center, almost out of the picture. The color scheme, too, is provocative and offbeat.*

The cool, almost monochromatic background is reminiscent of a Grenfell, and while the trees and background are similarly colored, the background is worked horizontally, the trees vertically. Another surprising element is the border, done in colors so subtle and close to one another that they almost blend together.

The owners, dealers in American antiques, chose to hang this rug over an early Log Cabin quilt made from light and dark satin strips. The starkness of the room allows each of the elements their full due.

Boy Scout Camp

Opposite: *This is an unusual subject for a hooked rug. The scout leader in full uniform is larger than life as he stands sentinel in front of the log cabin. The scouts are having a sail on the lake as the sun comes up over the mountains. This 20″ × 36″ rug owned by Susan Parrish is a rare find.*

W2QBP

Right: *It is hard to imagine what inspired the maker of this early rug. Perhaps it was an advertisement for a radio station or a business memento. The transmission lines between the towers are sending out strong signals from what looks like a rather remote area. Made in 1938, it measures 21″ × 35″.*

Justin's Whale Rug

Right: *Inspired by a whale watch, Jule Marie Smith made this 3′ × 5′ rug for her son in 1984. The pictorial border, which is harmonious with and enhances the inner subject, contains three different themes.*

Her materials were carefully chosen. For the sails, the artist used wool from a child's soft carriage blanket woven with wonderful speckles. For the turbulent sea, she dyed many strips of fabric in shades of blues and greens. The clouds were created from hues of white, off-white, blue/white, and green/white to suggest billows.

HOUSE WITH ROSES
Opposite: A charming early-twentieth-century rug shows out-of-scale objects, like the large flowers growing next to the house. Interior decorator Trudy Dujardin hung this delightful wallhanging in the dining room of a 1700s Connecticut house.

BY THE HEARTH
Left: This delightful rug pattern employs visual clichés that folk artists have adopted to express "hearth and home" in a fresh way. Stylized illustrations like this are frequently found in needlepoint patterns and cross-stitch samplers. 28″ × 45″

SAMPLER RUG
Left: A typical design from a cross-stitch sampler was adapted for this cheerfully primitive rug. Its graphic design makes it a decorative wall hanging, which at some time in the past may have served to instruct children in their ABCs. Sadly, the rug maker did not hook a date into the sampler that now resides in a child's bedroom filled with antique toys. A scale pattern for this rug appears on pages 148 to 149. 23″ × 40″

BOOKCASE
Right: Whether as a trompe l'oeil image on the wall or a surrealistic image on the floor, this unique rug holds up as a work of elegant design and color. Made by the Orton Jones Studio in 1940 of wool on burlap, it measures 92″ × 25½″ and was found in Connecticut. It is part of Barbara Johnson's collection.

Yesterday's Boys
Roslyn Logsdon concentrated on the repetition of patterns in this 20″ × 35″ rug.

Sandy Hook
Roslyn Logsdon's rug making technique has been inspired by the pointillism of the Impressionists in that each loop is but a dot that combines with the others to form an image. She uses a limited color palette that echoes the muted shades of old photographs. 35″ × 56″

CONVERSATION II

Roslyn Logsdon is a contemporary rug maker and weaver from Laurel, Maryland, whose work is exhibited in galleries all over the country. Her pictorial rugs contain elements of the past and something of the present.

The wallhanging illustrates the artist's preoccupation with relationships. Whether she depicts a couple at a table, a group of friends at the shore, or a team in front of the old school, her pieces are intimate and meant to reflect our collective history. This 16½" × 19" rug uses primarily tweed fabrics for texture and to achieve a play of light and shadow.

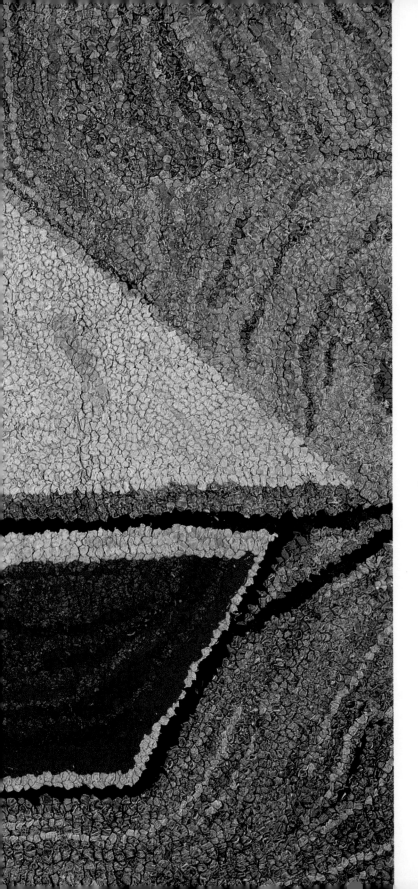

NAUTICAL THEMES

Many of the earliest hooked rugs that survive today come from maritime settlements. The long, inactive periods at sea led to the invention of all sorts of crafts, such as scrimshaw, macramé, and an early, primitive form of rug hooking in which sailors used bits of raveled burlap to create marine scenes on a rough linen ground. Early sailors' rugs often pictured ships, a motto, and the name of the vessel.

These early rugs looked as though they might have been hooked, but upon examination the hemp proved to be knotted into the linen with a marlinspike rather than hooked through it in loops. In all probability, true rug hooking as we define the craft evolved when a sailor's wife, admiring her husband's handwork, decided to use old materials in the house in a similar fashion. She soon discovered that knotting the material wasn't necessary and the work went faster if it was just pulled through in loops. Her subject matter, hearth and home, reflected her surroundings rather than those of her seafaring mate.

THE LARK
Dated 1875, this cotton and wool rug on burlap was found on Nantucket Island and might have been hooked by an early settler. The sweet little schooner is outlined against a background hooked to evoke the motion of the sea. Measuring 30½″ × 63″, the rug is part of Barbara Johnson's collection.

Setting Sail

This peaceful seaside picture is of a typical New England vista. To the people who live in this town, the church steeples, lighthouse, sailboats, and red buoy are familiar sights when entering the harbor. The 30" × 40" rug adds a cheerful touch to a greenhouse off the kitchen.

"Safe Harbor"

Opposite: *A late-nineteenth-century rug is mounted for hanging in this sunroom filled with nautical artifacts. It shows primitive sailboats and sticklike, barren trees on the mountains surrounding a cove. The water has been hooked in curves and gentle swells, giving this rug a three-dimensional perspective. Additional green ships dot the land area, perhaps in dry dock. The carved ivory canes and basket reside next to a "Boston Pavement" rug on the floor. 24" × 39"*

Clipper Ship "Great Republic"

Made between 1920 and 1930, the gray background of this ship portrait is hooked in vertical lines to set off the white sails. Curving lines of the same gray shade the undersides of the billowing sails. The rug's monochromatic tones blend with the dark wood floors and fieldstone fireplace to make a vignette that could easily have been found decades earlier in a Nantucket home. A floral hooked pad covers the seat of a wooden rocker. 35" × 50"

"Stern All, Pull Lads"
Whaling scenes like this one are often seen in paintings and scrimshaw pieces. For Nantucketers, this picture of a giant whale being captured by men in an oar-powered whale boat is an everpresent part of the island's history. Nantucket rug hooker Polly Miller has captured the excitement and peril of the chase in this oval rug, whose border boasts a symbolic oar and a harpoon.

FULL SAILS AHEAD
Homes on the New England coast and to the south are filled with seafaring memorabilia. This 26" × 31" mounted wallhanging is a fine example of the rug hooker's sense of color and playfulness. Notice the whale-shaped cloud in the sky. A scale pattern for this rug appears on pages 144 to 145.

GRENFELLS

The Grenfell Mission was established in the 1890s by Dr. Wilfred Grenfell, a physician devoted to relieving poverty, sickness, and exploitation along the northern coast of Newfoundland. The poor natives were gifted artisans who made distinctive hooked rugs depicting scenes of northern life.

In order to conserve materials, these rug makers used worn underwear and silk stockings that they cut into very narrow strips. This resulted in the dense, even pile characteristic of Grenfell rugs. There was a popular saying at the time, "When your stockings run, let them run to Labrador."

DOG TEAM
Left: Designed by an American, Stephen Hamilton, in 1939 for the Grenfell Mission, this rug was created with rayon or silk-stocking strips and cotton-knit fabric on burlap. The designer has effectively captured the lighting with shadows on the snow and a brilliant sky lit by the setting sun. We know this scene takes place at the end of a winter day. A black border frames this wallhanging, which is situated over a marble fireplace. A trio of carved ivory candlesticks are set to one side. 34" × 44¼"

FISH FLAKE
Right: Made in 1933 by Rhoda Dawson, this graphic wallhanging is appealing for its rhythmic lines and soft colors. The subject matter is vintage Grenfell Mission: codfish fillets. It hangs over a collection of original Shaker boxes on an early table in this Federal-style house. 26½" × 39½"

CALENDAR
Left: *Made in 1943, this rug was designed for a calendar that was sold by the Grenfell Mission. 19¼″ × 27″*

ARCTIC HUNTER
Opposite: *Bright colors, though used sparingly in Grenfells, enliven this male hunter's jacket. This typical scene shows everyday life in Newfoundland. Made in 1933, it measures 7¼″ × 9½″.*

HEADING HOME
Below: *This 27″ × 36″ rug shows an often repeated theme of Grenfells: a moon lighting the way for a hunter and his dog on their way toward a distant cabin.*

Grenfell organized the rug hookers and established a cottage industry in order to help the local people subsist over the long, bleak winters. These rugs were sold throughout the United States and did much to promote the craft of rug hooking.

Through expert marketing, the distinctive Grenfell rugs became much sought after and the Mission was highly successful from 1918 to the late 1930s. After World War II, materials became scarce and the industry faded. Today, many collectors favor these rugs, and from time to time they pop up at shows, flea markets, or in antiques stores. Even without their original Grenfell Mission labels, they are easily identified by their cool, monochromatic palette and graphic designs boldly outlined in black.

Welcome
The half-round Welcome mat was made in 1922. Unlike the cool-colored northern scenes, reddish colors and flowers make this rug distinctive. It is 24½" × 33".

St. Anthony's Harbor
Because this piece is small, it seems more colorful than most Grenfells. The red roofs of the houses look relatively bright against the cool blues and browns of the sailing port. The quilt is the Steeplechase pattern and was made in 1883 by a group of women in Brooklyn, New York. 8¼" × 9"

CIRCULAR DOG TEAM
Opposite: *The circular shape of this rug enabled the designer to create an animated scene that is quite charming. The red parka seems almost brilliant in contrast with the other, more muted shades in this piece. Made in the 1930s, this rug is 15" in diameter.*

LONE POLAR BEAR
Right: *The tightly woven background of horizontal lines, black outlining, and stark scene suggest the bleakness of the Newfoundland coast. 18½" × 30"*

ICEBOUND PUFFIN
Below right: *On August 6, 1983, Paula and Bill Laverty stumbled upon their first Grenfell, an illustration of a puffin, and it was love at first sight. That year, the Lavertys bought two more Puffins and began an ongoing quest for these distinctive rugs. Today they have an impressive collection and Paula has become involved with plans for the first exhibition of Grenfell rugs to be presented by the American Folk Art Museum in New York City. 7⅛" × 9⅝"*

STORYTELLING RUGS

Rugs that evoke personal images or memories, that impart a message, or are linked to family life are never ordinary. The messages found in these rugs range from the intensely personal to the profound or simple and straightforward. Some are quite humorous, while others have barbed or ironic messages hooked into them. Relatives by marriage, for example, were often the subject for humorous as well as spiteful sayings. Wives also vented emotions about their spouses in pictures and words, making these rugs among the earliest expressions of women's liberation.

Not all storytelling rugs carry an original legend. Some repeated a favorite line from a poem or song; others carried a phrase that described the illustration. Many "saying" rugs contain misspelled words, perhaps a reflection of the unwritten rule among early rug makers that accuracy yields to creative involvement.

The most common type of message rugs are the little "Welcome" mats placed by the door. These were always worked in a half circle to fit the sill of the door with the words worked across the bottom

Opposite: *Detail of Sailor rug on page 84*

SAILOR
"He'll Drain The Dregs Of Many Kegs And Come Up Smiling." This typical Hutchinson design is not an old rug. The original, owned by rug hooker Polly Miller, was too worn to repair, but she liked the design so much that she re-created it. The sailor's face can be seen in many Hutchinson rugs created in the 1920s.

edge. The individual designs are as varied as the makers, but the message is unmistakable.

"Home Sweet Home" hearth rugs were found by the fireplace in every nineteenth-century home. The lettering was often copied from a cross-stitch sampler and bore a resemblance to those careful creations. These message rugs have been made since rug hooking began and have never gone out of vogue.

Among the most important designers of storytelling rugs are James L. and Mercedes Hutchinson. The couple, who were reputed to have owned a circus in the 1920s, traveled a great deal and collected rugs along the way. These inspired Mr. Hutchinson to design humorous illustrations of his own, many incorporating phrases, which his wife drew onto burlap. The rugs were then hooked by the circus performers, friends, relatives, and whomever else they could enlist. Each one was unique and attested to the versatility and imagination of the designer. Many themes and even characters recur in Hutchinson rugs, which are greatly prized by collectors today and are often replicated by contemporary rug makers.

GENERAL WASHINGTON
This historic rug dated 1890 reads, "General Washington Noblest of Men His House His Horse His Cherry Tree & Him." Found in Richmond, Virginia, it measures 29" × 52½" and is part of Barbara Johnson's collection.

I LOVE MY GOOD MAN WITH A TENDER DEVOTOIN
BUT I CAN NOT GO HIS KIN !

LET LOVE BE YOUR GUIDE
Many storytelling rugs depict the act of elopement. This one, made between 1930 and 1940, is 29″ × 56″ and dominates center stage over the painted mantelpiece. As Cupid urges the couple toward the church, the woman leans blissfully against her beau, the horse gallops forward, and an angry protestor *is left waving wildly behind. The random swirls of hit-or-miss hooking create an energetic background. The reddish brown colors are beautifully rendered and, in contrast, the bride, Cupid, and church are soft and pristine.*

KIN
"I Love My Good Man With A Tender Devotoin But I Can Not Go His Kin!" This rug designed by James L. and Mercedes Hutchinson of Brooklyn, New York, in 1920 is made of wool, cotton, and rayon on burlap. It is unclear whether it was Mr. Hutchinson or the rug maker who was unable to spell devotion, *but* this type of charming flaw is found in many storytelling rugs. The mustached gentleman in the center is a familiar face in Hutchinson's rugs. Barbara Johnson Collection. 32″ × 53″

WELCOME MAT
*"A Back Door Guest Is
Always Best." Made by Polly
Miller, this rug shows a guest
coming up the path to her
house. Polly says, "I made this
for my back door because
everybody I know comes to the
back. Only salesmen come to
the front." A scale pattern for
this rug appears on pages 150
to 151.*

THE ELOPEMENT
*This rug from Barbara
Johnson's collection was
designed by James L. and
Mercedes Hutchinson in 1920.
It measures 27½" × 60" and
was found in Rhode Island.
Wild roses and the hit-or-miss
background further suggest the
uninhibited abandon of the
elopement scene.*

YOUNG RIDERS
"How Often Doth A Maid Provoke A Man To Play The Dunce." Polly Miller restored this early rug, which was owned by her family for more than fifty years. It is 36" × 56".

SUPPER TIME
An impatient husband waits for his supper while his wife cooks in the large fireplace. The wonderful details like the lace tablecloth, brick fireplace, and pastel border add to the delightful scene of a decidedly "unliberated" couple from the nineteenth century.

DESIGNS FROM THE GARDEN

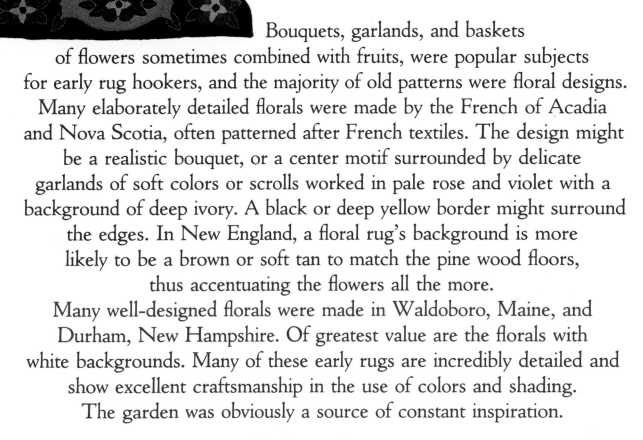

Bouquets, garlands, and baskets
of flowers sometimes combined with fruits, were popular subjects
for early rug hookers, and the majority of old patterns were floral designs.
Many elaborately detailed florals were made by the French of Acadia
and Nova Scotia, often patterned after French textiles. The design might
be a realistic bouquet, or a center motif surrounded by delicate
garlands of soft colors or scrolls worked in pale rose and violet with a
background of deep ivory. A black or deep yellow border might surround
the edges. In New England, a floral rug's background is more
likely to be a brown or soft tan to match the pine wood floors,
thus accentuating the flowers all the more.
Many well-designed florals were made in Waldoboro, Maine, and
Durham, New Hampshire. Of greatest value are the florals with
white backgrounds. Many of these early rugs are incredibly detailed and
show excellent craftsmanship in the use of colors and shading.
The garden was obviously a source of constant inspiration.

New England Bouquet
*Opposite: Detail of an early rug, New England Bouquet, made
with shades of pinks and violets against a pale green background.
The greatest workmanship is exhibited in the subtle shading used
to create the details in each flower.*

FRUITS AND FLOWERS

During the Victorian period, the illustrations of floral bouquets and theoremlike baskets of fruit were favorite subjects for the women who hooked rugs. Glorious blossoms, twining vines of grapes and leaves, and posylike bouquets were popular designs in wallpaper, furniture decorations, and ornamental moldings, and can all be seen reflected in the central motifs and borders of rugs of that period.

Many early rug hookers were partial to the oval shape for their designs. One often finds a bouquet or basket of flowers surrounded by a decorative border on such rugs.

PURPLE GRAPE VINE
In this nineteenth-century rug, subtle colors were employed to create a muted background for the realistic illustration of a grape vine. The unusual black and gray border adds to the interest of this 4' × 6' rug, which is uniquely suited to this early 1800s house. The worn, rich wood of the old floorboards, deacon's bench, and seed cabinet create a warm setting. Boat models, shore birds, and a lightship basket are a few of the sea-related objects that fill the room.

COUNTRY GARDEN

Left: *It's unusual to find a rug with such intense colors, although brilliant scarlets and occasionally green can be found in early as well as later rugs. The unusual deep, floral border on a black background adds to the overall effect and creates a frame for the center bouquet.*

This is a beautiful example of a rug made from early rug designer Mary Barstow's pattern of the 1890s. Mary Barstow patterns featured profusions of flowers and are still being reproduced today. This rug is 34″ × 65″ and was purchased in Nantucket for the owners' home in upstate New York. Shown here, on top of a deep green carpet in the bedroom, the red and green floral theme is echoed throughout.

FIELD OF FLOWERS

Right: *Red and white flowers grow in gay abandon over the field of gray in this twentieth-century rug. One sees lilies of the valley, daisies, roses, tulips, and an occasional butterfly. Interlocking circles, used to create a border on this oval shape, was a favorite design element of early rug makers.*

This rug and the more precise One-Inch Square geometric rug look especially fresh against a white painted floor. The Dresden Plate quilt and furniture of different periods add to the combination of interesting elements in this bedroom. The western-style bed was made by the owner, Ken Olsen. Approximately 38″ × 52″

FLOWER BASKET

Opposite: *Black was often used as a background to set off a pattern of bright florals. This design has a Pennsylvania Dutch feeling and is mounted over the mantel in a house built circa 1724. Called "Sunset Cottage," the house is listed in the historic and architectural survey of Fairfield, Connecticut, and interior designer Trudy Dujardin has furnished it in keeping with its character. This 20″ × 36″ early-twentieth-century wallhanging would have been just as appropriate a century ago. A scale pattern for this rug appears on pages 160 to 161.*

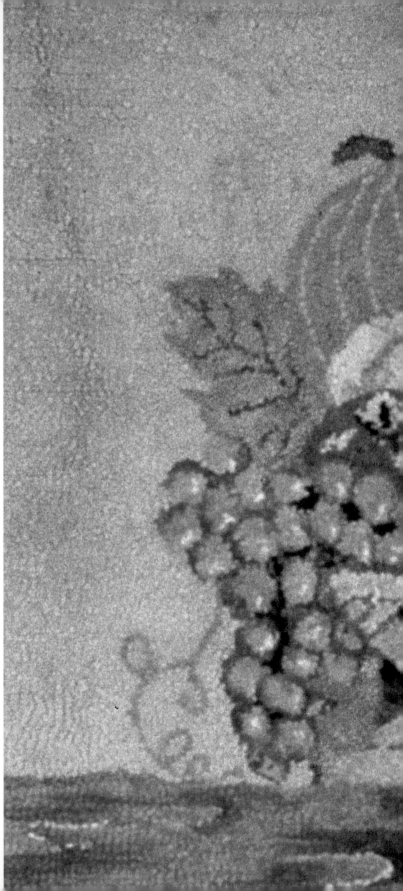

Basket of Fruit

Above and right: Stenciled designs painted on velvet were called "theorems," an art form popular in the nineteenth century. Copying was the accepted method of art study for female students who worked at this craft; originality of design was not the object.

This mounted rug hanging, patterned after a mid-nineteenth-century theorem painting, was made in Wisconsin. The addition of a braided border in matching colors frames the illustration and makes it quite elegant in a setting of early Nantucket lightship baskets and Connecticut stoneware crocks.

Found in Newburyport, Rhode Island, this New England rug of wool on burlap is 36″ × 45″.

ROOM-SIZE RUGS

Since room-size rugs were difficult to make, took hundreds of hours to complete, and required that several women work together, most were commissioned by studios rather than made by individuals and are quite rare.

Perhaps the best known of the custom rug studios was The Ruggery in Long Island, New York. The business was started by Mr. and Mrs. Alfred P. Porter after World War I and later sold to George Wells, who was active in the Arts and Crafts Movement of the 1950s. Wells designed personalized rugs and made them with hand-dyed wools just as the Porters had done. Wells died in 1988, but the company continues to make custom rugs under the ownership of James F. Beasley, a designer who joined the company in 1980. Their scarcity has made these large-scale pieces extremely coveted, and some collectors feel that no "important" collection is complete without at least one large rug.

WILDFLOWERS ON THE POND
Designed and made by George Wells in 1970, this 12′ × 8′ room-size rug is most unusual. Wildflowers grow around the pond, while colorful birds fly overhead. At right is a detail of a tern holding the "Wells' made" label on a corner of Wildflowers on the Pond.

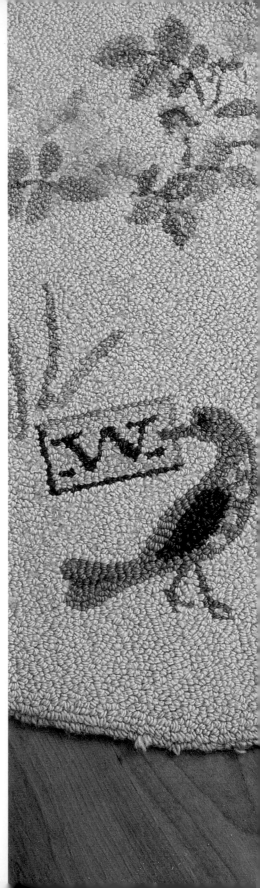

FLOWER POWER

Left and above: *A large
rug such as this, with its bold
design, becomes the dominant
force in a room. This rug was
made in upstate New York
in 1940 and measures
11½' × 16½'. Influences
from different patterns are
evident: acanthus-leaf scrolls,
Cape Cod florals, and
traditional scrolls. A detail of
Flower Power, left, shows the
creative application of a hit-or-
miss background. Its beige*

*tones set off the pastel flowers.
    The eclectic mix in this
bedroom shows the creative
personal style of the owner. A
crewel-embroidered Victorian
sofa resides next to a basket
holding an 1890 Fan pattern
crazy quilt. The antique wicker
rocker is filled with patchwork
pillows made from scraps of
old quilts and the bed is an
unusual antique, thought to be
a plantation bed. The primitive
bathroom door came from a
Pennsylvania outhouse.*

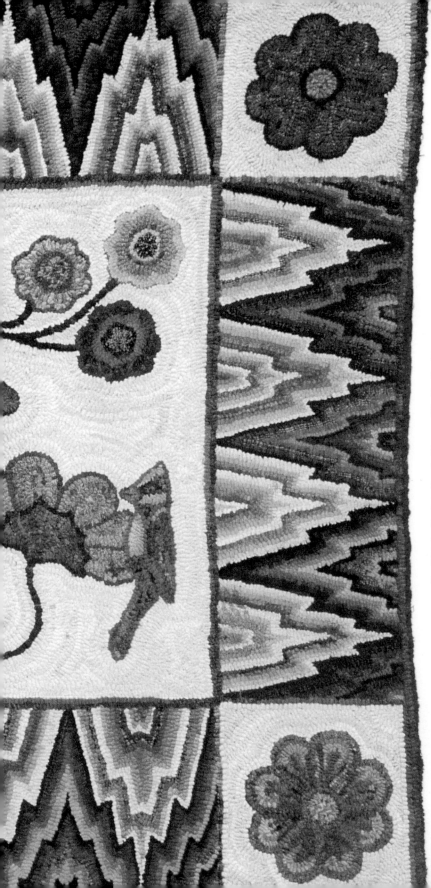

GEOMETRIC FLORALS

Rugs combining a pattern of squares with alternating patterns of flowers were a step beyond the simple geometric rugs. These rugs bear a striking resemblance to appliqué quilts in which floral blocks alternate with pieced blocks.

Alternating squares of florals and geometrics gave the rug maker an opportunity to be creative with the placement and arrangement of patterns, use up leftover scraps, and make the rug any size. Beginners liked this type of rug because each square, when finished, afforded a sense of accomplishment. The plain areas would have been boring if they weren't so small and, as each was finished, a floral or leaf square offered a change of pace.

SUNFLOWER AND FLAME
This 4' × 5½' rug was created by Jule Marie Smith, who grows sunflowers in her garden each year. She used many golden tweeds in the center of the giant sunflower to simulate the nubby rows of seeds. The colors in this rug were overdyed in onionskins, which have a bronzy mellowing effect. The flame border makes this rug quite elegant. The center motif against the white background is reminiscent of crewel embroidery and the flame border is similar to needlepoint designs.

INTERLOCKING
HALF CIRCLE

Popular among geometrics is the broken or interlocking circle. This pattern, often used on runners, was also called Fish Scale or Shell and is reminiscent of cobblestones. Sometimes this pattern was rendered in bright colors, but the most pleasing examples are those with faded tones. This unusually long runner resembles a flower-strewn street. The subtle colors make it both practical and a soft contrast to the tile floor in this sunroom.

GRANDMOTHER'S FLOWER GARDEN

This sweet little rug represents the most basic type of floral geometric: a simple checkerboard grid of textured squares alternating with floral squares. It measures 28″ × 54″.

ROSE OF SHARON

Following spread: *Roses are the flowers found most often in hooked rugs. They can be quite realistic or highly stylized. In this 25″ × 50″ rug made between 1940 and 1950, Annette Stackpole used a pattern popular with early rug hookers.*

Many crafters devised their own interpretation and color scheme, often based on the materials they had at hand. Rarely, however, did a rug maker create a rose that wasn't true to its colors. Most roses are hooked in reds and pinks or occasionally yellow.

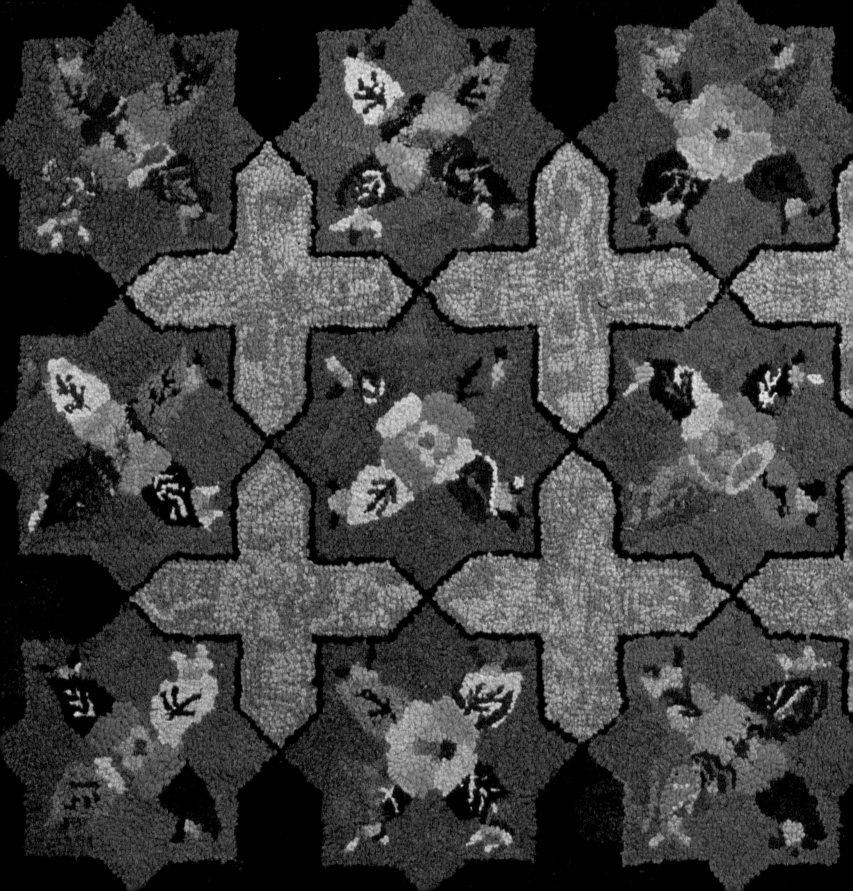

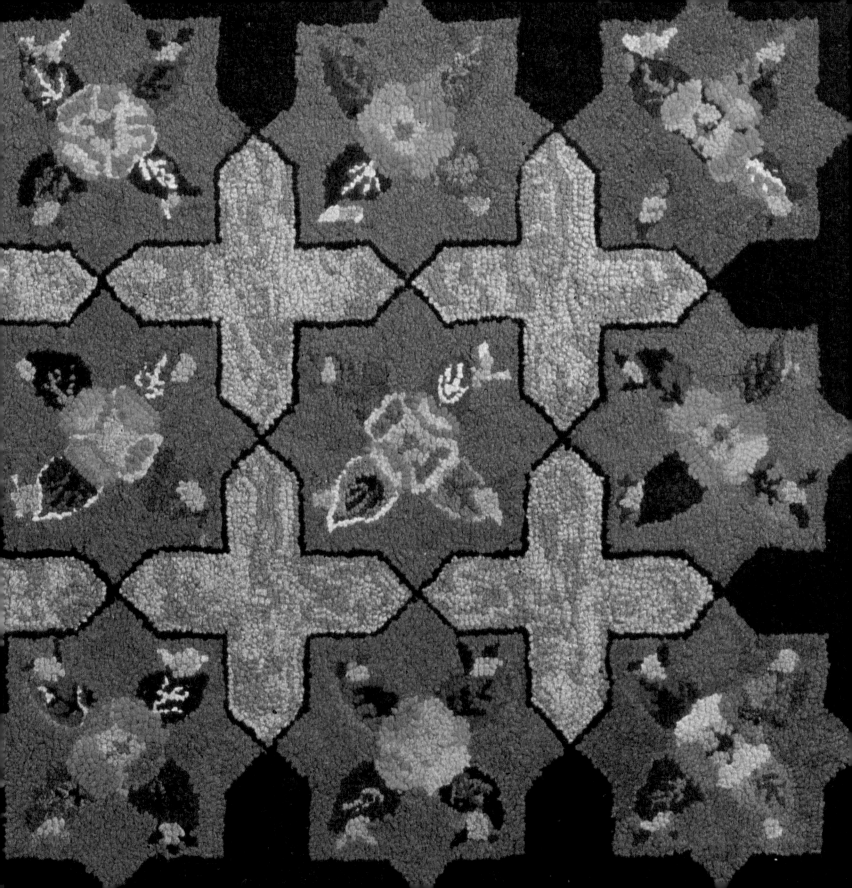

FLOWERS AND LEAVES
This colorful rug brightens the end of a hallway filled with antique furniture and painted boxes. A collection of early metal banks lines the top of the antique apothecary chest.

BLOCK PRINTS
This floral geometric has an art nouveau feeling, and while the rug has been in use since the 1940s, the colors remain bright. The placement of vertical and horizontal alternating blocks was a common use of a basic hit-or-miss pattern. The predominantly red colors against a black background give this rug, made by Annette Stackpole, a modern look. A scale pattern for this rug appears on pages 154 to 155. 34" × 49"

SCROLL BORDERS

Most floral designs consisted of one or more borders surrounding a floral arrangement. A popular type of border incorporated scroll shapes similar to the designs carved on Tudor furniture, while others looked like leaves or feathers. The rugs had names like Belmont Scroll and Barstow Scroll, named after the original designers, or Victorian Scroll.

According to Pearl McGown, who is credited with the revival of traditional rug hooking, New England women often made paper patterns of favorite scrolls from wallpaper, furniture, or magazine illustrations, which they adapted for border designs in their rugs. Leaves are used extensively in hooked-rug designs and they are always seen with flowers. As a border, they can often overpower the flowers they surround. The acanthus leaf is a favorite for a continuous border and is often made with light and dark colors.

VICTORIAN URN
Folk art collector Rubens Teles has hooked rugs throughout his three-story house and feels there's no sense in collecting rugs if they're too precious for everyday use. Geometrics, florals, pictorials, and animals all work well with his other folk art pieces. The flower urn rug has a Victorian scroll border and is an adaptation of an early pattern. It measures 30″ × 60″ and was skillfully repaired by the owner's mother. The other rugs are based on early geometric quilt patterns.

New England Bouquet
Left: *This pale oval rug quietly complements the Victorian decor in a sitting room. A scale pattern appears on pages 152 to 153.*

Matching Scrolls
Below left: *The two matching scroll rugs in this hallway are similar, but not identical. Old-fashioned red roses are often emphasized with black outlining in antique rugs. The owner thinks they might have been French Acadian rugs, which were rendered in a realistic style and often employed bright colors. These are 26″ × 62″.*

Leaf Scroll
Top right: *The pattern for this rug originated in the mid to late 1800s and many similar rugs have survived. Made with a particularly pretty color combination of autumn hues, this rug measures 52″ × 66″.*

Matching Florals
Right: *A set of matching hooked rugs covers the floor in this country bedroom. The rugs, which would be bland in another setting, add to the serene effect of the room. Patterned rugs such as these, combining flowers and leaf borders, were popular in the mid to late eighteen hundreds.*

Acanthus
Opposite: *The crafter of this rug probably created the central motif of roses and then adapted one of her scroll patterns for the border. The subtle tones blend perfectly with the other early folk art pieces in this hallway.*

ANIMALS AND BIRDS

An endless procession of household pets has been immortalized by devoted owners in hooked portraits. Early rug makers honored their favorite cats, dogs, cows, pigs, hens, and horses. In the nineteenth and early twentieth centuries, horses were central to daily life, both as transportation and farm labor and for recreational purposes. As a result, they are the subject of countless early rugs. Birds were also common subjects for rug hookers, since they were often easy to draw and inspiration could be found merely by gazing out one's window. Further, it was easy to find pictures of exotic birds in magazines and books. The American eagle figured prominently in patriotic rugs.

Pictorial rugs have always been sought after. Within this category, animal rugs are the most popular and command high prices, the most desirable being original rugs made from naive drawings.

Opposite: Detail of Partridge in a Pear Tree (see page 127). We can see how, prior to being walked upon, every loop of a new rug stands up. As the rug is used, the loops flatten down, tightening the pressure between the loops and making them more secure. It also changes the overall image slightly. A rug hooker must visualize, to some degree, what the design will look like in use.

CAT

*If one imagines the cat
vanishing from this rug, what is
left is a formal abstract design
done in warm subtle hues.
Upon this background sits a
cat whose form fits perfectly in
the center panel but whose
expression says, "What am I
doing here?" This is a
marvelous naive drawing and
an excellent example of early
folk art. The one-of-a-kind
mustard painted table is
thought to have been a dry sink
or dresser made between 1820
and 1830.*

KITTENS ON THE HEARTH

Many versions of this rug, made from a prestenciled pattern dating to before 1880, have been discovered, and are frequently mistaken for an original design. However, the colors, the border, the lettering, the flowers, the little mat, and the background offered opportunity for individual interpretation. A scale pattern for this rug appears on pages 156 to 157. 24" × 32"

FLORA'S KITTY

This little Persian cat was hooked and then cut out and appliquéd onto a hit-or-miss background. 24" × 29"

SPOTTED PIG
Unlike many animal rugs by artists and designers, this one is not highly stylized or decorative. The original colors of black, white, gray, and red are as basic as the design itself. It is a realistically rendered portrait of a big pig on a small rug by someone who knew what a real pig looks like. No doubt, familiarity inspired the rug maker. 20" × 35"

PIG AND PIGLETS
Newborn piglets wait their turn to feed. The fat mama pig practically fills the frame of this early-twentieth-century rug from Barbara Johnson's collection. Scotch plaid wool strips were used to create the black and red border. 26" × 46"

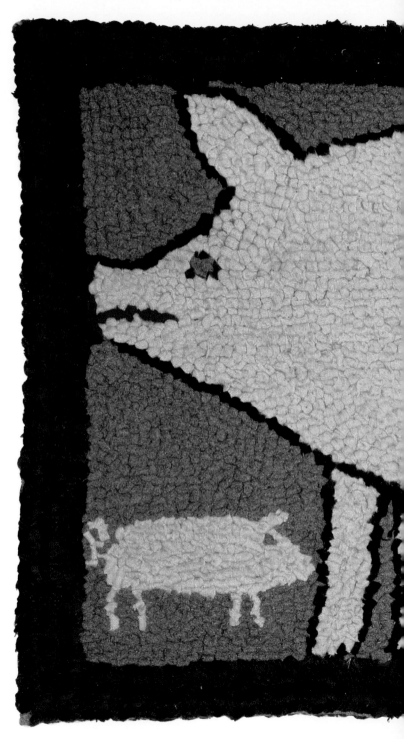

"THE DOG AND CAT"
This naive illustration of a dog and a cat was created by contemporary rug hooker Jon Swan in 1989. It is reminiscent of early animal designs.

KITTEN WITH SHOE
In this Jazz Age rug, made between 1930 and 1940, a peppy little feline plays with her mistress's red party shoe while the background bubbles with pink and lavender balls. The rug in its entirety appears on page 164.

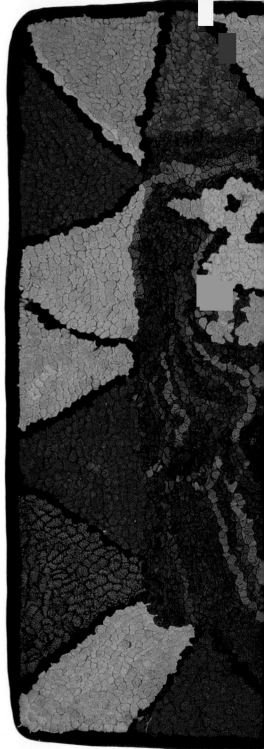

RED PARROT

Preceding spread, right:
This 30" × 45" rug is an example of Waldoboros, a unique type of rug hooking developed by German settlers in Waldoboro, Maine, during the nineteenth century. A combination of traditional hooking methods with a sculptured form of rug making, Waldoboros often have a raised effect achieved by cutting the pile at varied lengths. Typical Waldoboros played a bright floral arrangement against a dark background, but in this unusual example the raised central motif contrasts with a light background.

Preceding spread, left:
Detail of Red Parrot shows the high pile and rich details in contrast to the subtle background.

WHITE DUCK

This simple illustration, while accurately drawn, could have been done by a child. Except for the black outline of the duck, this rug was hooked almost entirely in shades of white, almost never used in hooked rugs. The duck is surrounded by a checkerboard pattern, giving it a contemporary country look. Preservation is one reason to wall-mount a rug that is too old and delicate for continued use on the floor. 20" × 31"

VIA PUMPKIN PATCH

Dated 1890, this adorable naive illustration was hooked with wool and cotton rag on burlap and measures 26" × 40". It was found in Connecticut and is part of Barbara Johnson's collection.

BUTTERFLIES ARE FREE

Opposite: Butterflies and other insects are rarely found in hooked rug designs. This one may have been inspired by an appliqué quilt pattern. Various appliqué quilts used colorful butterflies in design units of four. In this colorful adaptation, the result looks like a floral rug. 36" × 38"

PARTRIDGE IN A PEAR TREE

Top right: Designer Tish Murphy made this seasonal Welcome mat in 1989. The wintry colors are beautifully shaded to give the fruit and bird a three-dimensional quality. The pattern of hooking, which follows the curves of the design elements, adds to the interest. Holly leaves and berries create a delicate border. Modern rug makers are often more proficient and have more control over the medium than early rug makers, and their work is exquisitely rendered. The half round, wool on monk's cloth rug is 23" × 49".

EAGLE

Right: This is another rug by the mental patient who made Heart, Home, and Cross on page 37. In this rug, the artist uses primary symbols from religion and heraldry. It is unusual to find a religious symbol on a rug, since rug makers felt it was sacrilegious to walk on a cross. The eagle and the cross, the bright colors, and the unselfconscious quality create a dynamic image in this twentieth-century rug. 26" × 31"

Dear Deer

Left: *Autumn colors create a border around a simple illustration of two deer facing each other, a design that appears in old as well as newer rugs. A bare, brown tree in back of each deer is the only detail on the black background. The 28" × 36" rug hangs over the fireplace in this landmark Connecticut house. The designer, Trudy Dujardin, chose scrubbed pine furniture and a pencil post bed for this light and airy bedroom.*

Ram

Right: *The tightly composed design on this primitive round rug suggests Aries the ram surrounded by the moon and stars. While it appears to have been made with just one dark and one light color, the stars might have been much brighter. The purple and red colors have faded almost completely and the loops are practically flat, attesting to the rug's early origin. It was made in the 1870s and found in White Creek, New York, where it had resided for generations. 36" in diameter*

Stable Boy
Both the horse and the boy are looking out at the viewer in this early-twentieth-century rug. The simple shapes are fashioned with an economy of line and shape against a plain gray ground. The side decorations are made from dark solids and tweeds.

Primitive Pony
The vibrant background of this rug looks almost like a spontaneous crayon sketch. The texture contrasts with the basic silhouette of the pony. Like many primitive rugs, this one has a single design element placed against a background.

Pennsylvania Horse
Opposite: *Dated 1909, this rug found in Pennsylvania is an exquisite piece of folk art and serves as a dynamic wallhanging at one end of this room. The rug maker had a wonderful sense of color and design that evokes all sorts of speculation. Note the two irregular squares in the border on the right side. 43" × 50"*

ZACH'S PONY
Few rugs are as lively as this one. The horse is rearing in the barnyard where other animals, such as a pig and a rooster, appear quite small, as do the two buildings, the trees, and the farmer. The swirling pattern of the dark background adds to the excitement of this nineteenth-century rug. It measures 28" × 58"

"BRASS MONKEY"
This portrait of "Brass Monkey" is a realistic illustration of a favorite racehorse as he might have looked in the Winner's Circle. 30" × 44"

PUTTING IT
TOGETHER

COLLECTING HOOKED RUGS

Perhaps more than any other factor, collectors of hooked rugs are charmed and intrigued by their naive and simplistic designs. Since even the oldest hooked rugs date only from the mid-1800s, knowledgeable dealers admit that a rug's age is often less significant than its design. Collectors and dealers may have different opinions about which rugs are most valuable, but they are all in agreement when advising the would-be collector: Buy only what is personally appealing. Many collectors believe that if a rug lifts your spirits, that is reason enough to own it.

Barbara Johnson, one of the country's most prominent collectors of hooked rugs, says she is not interested in how a rug was made or with what material. Her only concern is its aesthetic value. When buying a rug, she wants to know that she can live with it for a long time. Since her environment is crammed with collections of all sorts, each rug must have an assertive personality or it will disappear in the space. While some collectors feel the rugs are too precious to place on the floor and suggest mounting or framing them, Ms. Johnson says, "If you elevate a piece of art beyond its own ambition, you don't do it a favor."

It is obvious from looking at auction prices that American folk art and, most recently, hooked rugs are escalating in price. George Korn, an antiques dealer specializing in early American folk art, advises collectors about selecting hooked rugs as a good investment, if this is their desire: "Perhaps rugs are now old enough for us to realize their real value as charming examples of early handwork and, as such, have increased in monetary value."

There are many sources for buying antique rugs. You can still find rugs at reasonable prices through auctions, flea markets, and yard sales. However, as often happens with other collectibles, dealers are aware of what is becoming valuable and they look for these items. Whether the rug comes from a country auction or a respected dealer, always buy the best you can afford. Korn says this will set a barometer for future acquisitions. He advises buyers to assess each new purchase in terms of their last; if it is not of equal or better quality, he counsels, pass it by. There will always be another.

Korn says that most serious collectors have their earliest purchased pieces stored away. These may not be the best rugs the collector owns. If you have rugs that aren't your favorites, upgrade your collection by selling these and using the money to buy better pieces.

Figurative rugs are usually the most expensive, but if they aren't in good condition and can't be repaired, they aren't worth buying. When purchasing a rug, look for uniqueness of design and pleasing colors. Sometimes the colors will have faded,

MERMAIDS

This primitive design in Barbara Johnson's collection may have been created by a lonely sailor who was not altogether unaware of women's ways. Above this, a rare Clouds rug hangs in a carefully arranged corner of the collector's living room. Made in 1880 of wool and cotton rag on burlap, it was purchased in New York and measures 32½" × 60½". Pig and Piglets on the coffee table is also shown on page 118.

and this can be very nice. Don't think that because a rug has faded that it isn't valuable. This may indicate that the rug is quite old and possibly rare. Rugs that were part of a well-known collection are often deemed valuable because they are more likely to be accompanied by documentation and are inevitably of extremely high quality.

A rug that is used on the floor will last longer and stay in better condition if you place it on top of another carpet or use a rubber pad beneath it. Keep valuable and delicate rugs out of high-traffic areas. Dirt, mud, spills, and sunlight are enemies of your hooked rugs. If you find a wonderful old rug that is too delicate to use, it can be bound and mounted for framing. There are good restorers who can mend rugs and mount them for you.

And finally a word about new hooked rugs. If you want to decorate with them, take the time to become knowledgeable about the craft. There are good contemporary rug hookers. Find a designer whose work appeals to you, and again, buy the best you can afford.

*The walls, floors, and even ceilings in collector Barbara Johnson's home house an impressive collection of hooked rugs. At **left,** the central rug is dynamic and complex. It is a visual composition that compels the viewer to look for forms and images of real things that may or may not be there. The rug above it to the right has a similar quality. It could be the early rug hooker's expression of abstract art as we know it in the twentieth century or merely a hit-or-miss rug. **Right:** Mosaic in quality, this early rug in Barbara Johnson's dining room might have been patterned after a crazy quilt. The Reindeer in front and the Frog on Lily Pad beyond are right at home with the collector's mélange of other folk art collectibles and plants.*

CARE, REPAIR, AND RESTORATION

Many rugs have been lost to future generations of appreciators by unknowing souls who tossed them out, unaware that old rugs, even those in bad condition, can often be restored. If the restorer is experienced, even the most discerning collector can't always tell where the old and the new meet.

Many collectors, dealers, museums, and fine auction houses send their rugs to be reclaimed by Marianne Swan, who has been responsible for restoring some of the most beautiful rugs in the country.

Her Great Barrington, Massachusetts, studio brims with strips of old wool in every color imaginable, allowing her to match repairs perfectly.

If you have a rug that needs restoring, it's important to find a qualified expert. Restorers like Marianne Swan often begin by taking out repairs done on rugs before they reached their workrooms. Swan suggests that it helps if the restorer is a fine sewer. She attributes her expert craftsmanship in rug restoration to her background in haute couture.

Some rugs, however, are truly beyond repair. If you fall in love with a rug that isn't in perfect condition, Swan suggests holding it up to the light. If it's filled with holes, it may have dry rot, a sure sign that it will eventually fall apart. This sort of disrepair is impossible to fix. On the other hand, if it is just frayed or has a small hole, it may be worth preserving.

For routine maintenance, don't vacuum the rug, but rather place it face down and use a brush to sweep it. (Some people suggest cleaning a rug by placing it face down on newly fallen, powdery snow, then brushing it off to remove dirt. Not everyone agrees that this method works, but it's worth trying.) If a more thorough washing is needed, do a section at a time using a soft brush and cold, slightly soapy water. Do not wring the rug or hang it up to dry. Instead, with the right side up, roll the rug in a heavy towel to absorb the moisture, then lay it flat to dry.

When your rug needs a deep cleaning, it is important that you send it to a dry cleaner that specializes in cleaning hooked rugs and knows how to handle them with care; the harsh chemicals and rough handling used by conventional dry cleaners can damage or fade a delicate rug.

Sunning and airing rugs from time to time is a good idea, but never shake a rug. If it is very old, it may fall apart right in your hands. The burlap in old rugs tends to be so much weaker than the wool that it often disintegrates.

Sometimes it's best to hang a delicate and valuable rug on the wall, rather than use it on the floor. It's important to mount a rug carefully and properly for even weight distribution. There are professionals who will mount the piece without damaging it (see Resources, page 164).

When storing a rug, never fold it or put it in an airtight plastic bag. It is best to roll it with the front side out and wrap it with a sheet or cloth for protection.

Detail of meticulous restoration being done on an early rug in Marianne Swan's studio.

RUG PATTERNS TO MAKE

It can be fun to design your own hooked rug based on a favorite scene, pattern, or motif. Some rug hookers, however, are not confident of their ability to draw a suitable illustration. And first-time rug makers often appreciate the security of following a pattern.

The patterns provided on the pages that follow are easy to re-create and offer a variety of subject matter. A geometric design is usually the easiest to copy and therefore a good choice for a first project. You can refer to the finished rugs in the front of this book in order to choose your colors, or you can make the rug uniquely your own by experimenting with different color schemes. If you are unsure how the finished project will look, use colored pencils to fill in the design on your tracing before beginning the hooking process.

Enlarging Designs

Because of space limitations, the patterns on the pages that follow have been reduced and must be enlarged to the correct size before they are transferred to a fabric backing for hooking. To simplify enlargement, the designs are shown on a grid.

To transfer a rug design to your base material, you will need a sheet of paper at least as large as the dimensions of the finished rug you will be making. Rule off a grid to the size specified. Make sure the number of squares on the large grid corresponds to the number of squares on the pattern you are copying. Copy the design onto your grid one square at a time until the entire design has been reproduced. You are now ready to transfer the full-size design onto the backing fabric (see page 18). To enlarge Maltese Cross (see page 146) and House with Path (see page 162), use a ruler and sharp pencil to draw lines across the pattern, connecting the grid lines. Then follow the directions for copying the design as indicated above.

A 1920 stenciled pattern on burlap
indicates placement of color.
A scale pattern for this
design appears on pages 158 to 159.

Full Sails Ahead
courtesy of Forager House Collection (page 73).
Each square equals 1 inch.

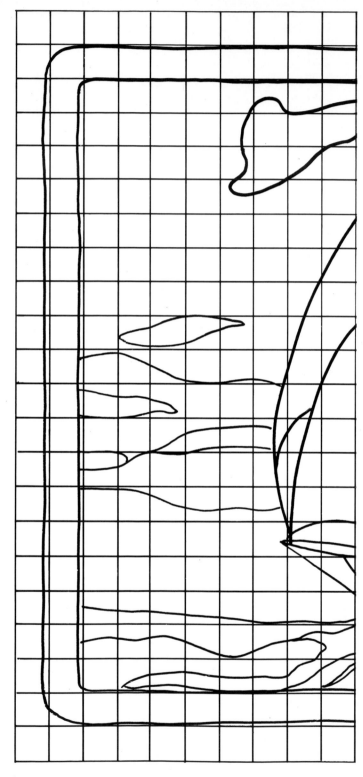

Putting It Together
145

Maltese Cross
courtesy Forager House Collection (pages 34 to 35).
Each square equals 1 inch.

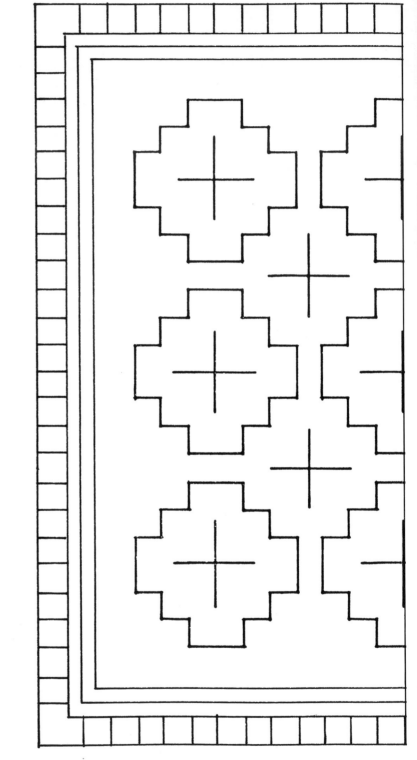

Sampler Rug
courtesy Betty and Kenneth Olsen (page 65).
Each square equals 2 inches.

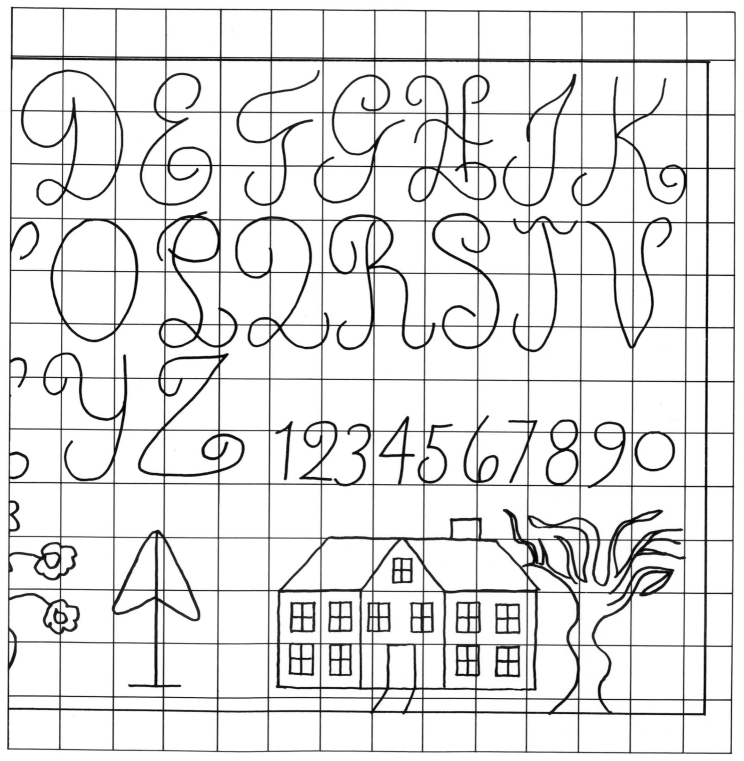

Welcome Mat
by Polly Miller (page 88).
Each square equals 1 inch.

New England Bouquet
courtesy Trudy Dujardin (pages 90 and 112).
Each square equals 2 inches.

Block Prints
by Annette Stackpole (page 109).
Each square equals 2 inches.

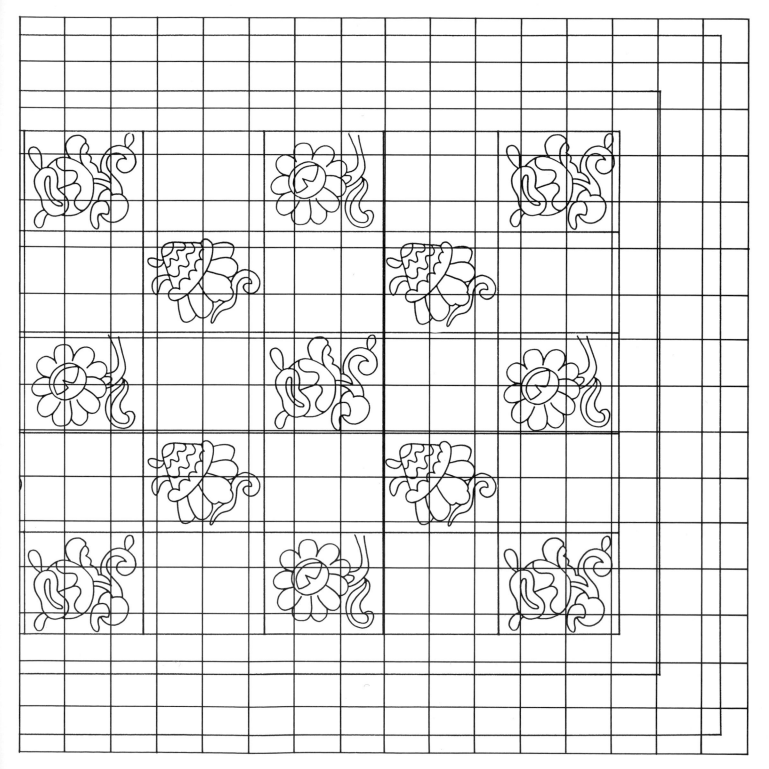

Kittens on the Hearth
courtesy Avis Skinner (page 117).
Each square equals 2 inches.

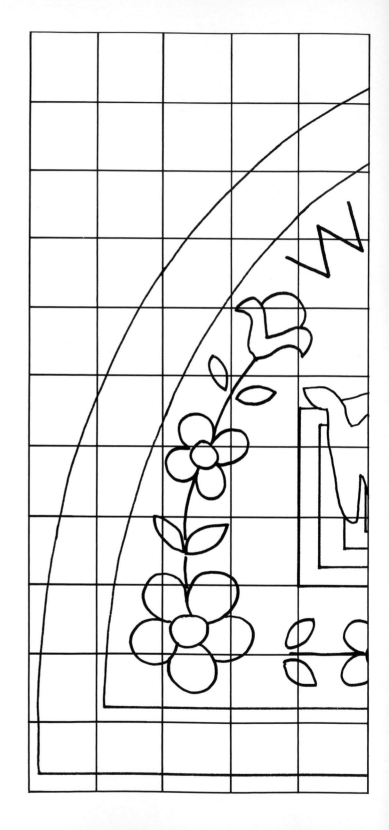

A 1920 stenciled pattern
courtesy Marianne Swan (pages 142 to 143).
Each square equals 2 inches.

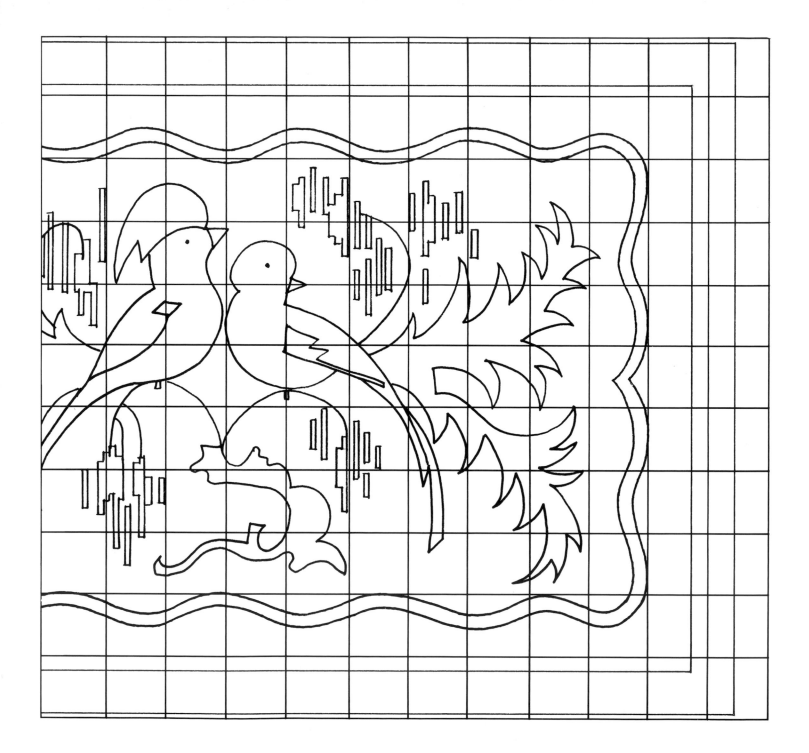

Flower Basket
courtesy Corrinne Burke (page 95).
Each square equals 2 inches.

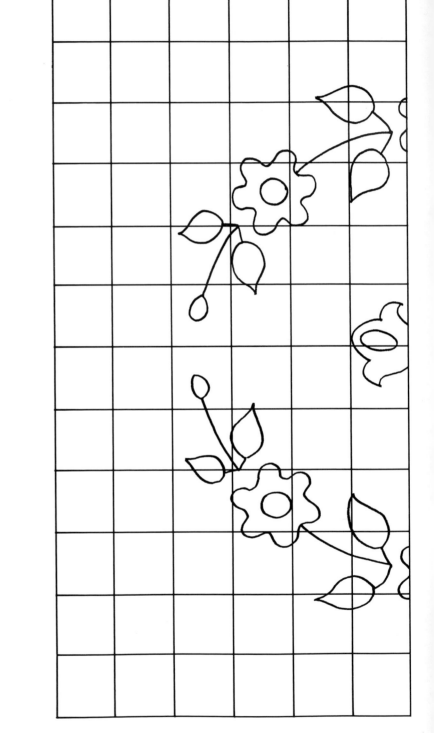

House with Path
courtesy Forager House Collection
(page 60). Each square equals 2 inches.

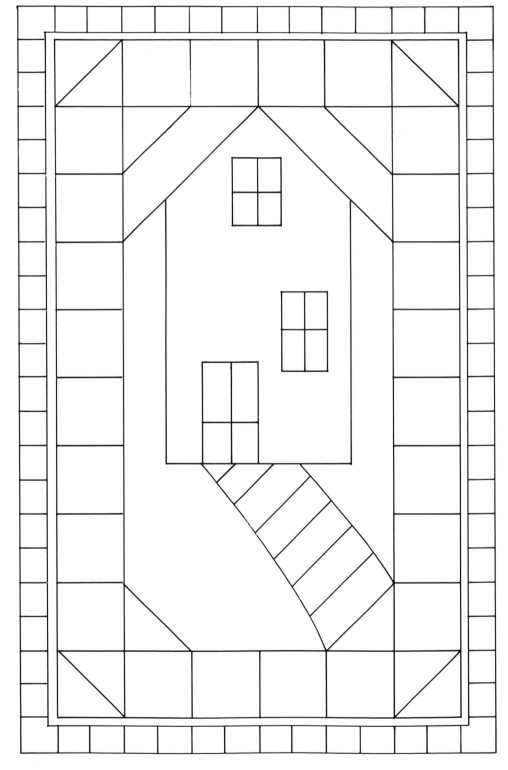

DIRECTORY

RESOURCES

CONSULTANTS AND DEALERS

American Hurrah Antiques
766 Madison Avenue
New York, NY 10021
(212) 535-1930
American folk art

Art Underfoot, Inc.
12 Godfrey Road
Upper Montclair, NJ 07043
(201) 744-4171
Representing contemporary rug hookers

Corinne Burke
PO Box 26
Goldens Bridge, NY 10526
(914) 232-7133
Antiques dealer

Helaine and Burton Fendelman
1248 Post Road
Scarsdale, NY 10583
(914) 725-0292
Appraisers and consultants on art, antiques, and collectibles

Forager House Collection
Summer:
20 Centre Street
Nantucket, MA 02554
(508) 228-5977
Winter:
PO Box 82
Washington Crossing, PA 18977
(215) 493-3007
Antiques, folk and fine art, consultants

Jay Johnson American Folk
    Heritage Gallery
1044 Madison Avenue
New York, NY 10021
(212) 628-7280
American folk art

Paul Madden Antiques
146 Main Street
Sandwich, MA 02563
(508) 888-6434
Antiques

Nantucket Looms
16 Main Street
Nantucket, MA 02554
(508) 228-1908
Contemporary rugs by
Polly Miller

The Packet Shop
1 Old South Wharf
Nantucket, MA 02554
(508) 228-4872
Miniature items for collectors

Susan Parrish
390 Bleecker Street
New York, NY 10014
(212) 645-5020
American folk art and quilts

James Richardson Gallery
Southport, CT
(203) 226-0358
Antiques dealer

Grace and Elliot Snyder
Box 598
South Egremont, MA 01258
(413) 528-3581
American antiques

Marianne Swan
292 Main Street
Great Barrington, MA 01230
(413) 528-3231
Restorer

Vis-A-Vis
34 Main Street
Nantucket, MA 02554
(508) 228-9102
Antique rugs and quilts

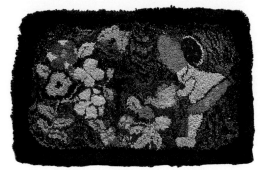

RUG-HOOKING SUPPLIES

Braid-Aid
466 Washington Street
Pembroke, MA 02359
(617) 826-6091
Wool, cutters, rug backings and
foundations

W. Cushing & Company
Joan Moshimer's Studio
PO Box 351
North Street
Kennebunkport, ME 04046
(207) 967-3711
Dyes

Davidson's Old Mill Yarn
PO Box 8
Eaton Rapids, MI 48827
(517) 663-2711
Wool rug yarns

The Dorr Mill Store
PO Box 88
Guild, NH 03754
(603) 863-1197
Wool yardage, burlap

Frederick J. Fawcett, Inc.
1304 Scott Street
Petaluma, CA 94954
(707) 762-3362
Linens

George Wells Rugs, Inc.
565 Cedar Swamp Road
Glen Head, NY 11545
(516) 676-2056
Wool, supplies

Harry M. Fraser Co.
R & R Machine Co., Inc.
192 Hartford Road
Manchester, CT 06040
(203) 649-2304
Supplies, cutters

Heirloom Rugs
Designs of Louise Hunter
   Zeiser
28 Harlem Street
Rumford, RI 02916
Catalog of patterns printed on
burlap

Henry Ford Museum and
   Greenfield Village
PO Box 1970
Dearborn, MI 48121
Edward Frost original rug
stencils and hooked rug
collection

Jacqueline L. Hansen
237 Pine Point Road
Scarborough, ME 04074
207-883-5403
Traditional and primitive rug
patterns

ORGANIZATIONS

American Craft Council
40 West 53rd Street
New York, NY 10019
Membership information:
(212) 274-0630

Association of Traditional
   Hooking Artists (ATHA)
c/o Celeste Schifino
Membership Chairperson
103 Glen Meadow Road
Franklin, MA 02038
(617) 528-7077

National Guild of Pearl
   McGown, Inc.
c/o Jane McGown Flynn
Box 1301
Sterling, MA 01564

Ontario Hooking Craft Guild
Molly Marks
Membership Convenor
Suite 326, 25 Austin Drive
Unionville, ONT L3R 8H4
Canada
(416) 479-5271

PERMANENT COLLECTIONS OF HOOKED RUGS

The Bybee Collection
Dallas Art Museum
1717 North Harwood
Dallas, TX 75201
(214) 922-1200

The Henry Ford Museum
20900 Oakwood Boulevard
PO Box 1970
Dearborn, MI 48121-1970
(313) 271-1620

Shelburne Museum
Route 7
PO Box 10
Shelburne, VT 05482
(802) 985-3344

Society for the Preservation of
    New England Antiquities
    (SPNEA)
Beauport House
75 Eastern Point Boulevard
Gloucester, MA 01930
(508) 283-0800

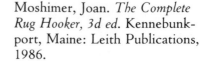

SELECTED READING

BOOKS

Bishop, Robert, and William Secord. *Quilts, Coverlets, Rugs and Samplers.* New York: Alfred A. Knopf, 1982.

Crouse, Gloria E. *Hooking Rugs: New Materials, New Techniques.* Newtown, Conn.: The Taunton Press, 1990.

Kent, William Winthrop. *Rare Hooked Rugs.* Springfield, Mass.: Pond-Ekberg Co., 1941.*

Kopp, Joel, and Kate Kopp. *American Hooked and Sewn Rugs.* New York: E. P. Dutton, 1985.

McGown, Pearl K. *The Dreams Beneath Design.* Boston: Bruce Humphries, Inc., 1939.*

Moshimer, Joan. *The Complete Rug Hooker, 3d ed.* Kennebunkport, Maine: Leith Publications, 1986.

Rex, Stella Hay. *Practical Hooked Rugs.* New York: Prentice Hall, 1949.*

Underhill, Vera Bisbee. *Creating Hooked Rugs.* New York: Coward-McCann, Inc., 1951.*

Waugh, Elizabeth, and Edith Foley. *Collecting Hooked Rugs.* New York: The Century Co., 1927.*

* These out-of-print books may be found in libraries. They are a good source of information, local color, and designs before 1950.

PERIODICAL

Rug Hooking
PO Box 15760
Harrisburg, PA 17105

CREDITS

Rugs by Barbara E. Merry:
pages 8–9, 56–57, 58 top

Courtesy of Harold and Judith
Huestine: page 89 top

Courtesy of Trudy Dujardin:
pages 90, 112 top left and
bottom right, 152

Courtesy of Corrinne Burke:
frontispiece, pages 64, 95, 128,
160

Courtesy of Marianne Swan:
pages 10, 59, 120, 141, 142–
143, 158

Courtesy of Paula and William
Laverty: pages 2, 42, 54, 74–81,
134–135

Courtesy of Barbara Johnson
Collection: pages 25, 38–39,
46–47, 65 right, 68–69, 83, 85,
87, 88 bottom, 119, 125, 137,
138, 139

Courtesy of Forager House
Collection: pages 13, 17, 26, 28,
31 top, 34–35, 37, 49 bottom,
60, 63 top, 71, 73, 91, 120, 124,
126, 127 bottom, 130 top, 132,
133 right, 144, 146, 154, 162,
164 left, 165 left

Rugs by Annette Stackpole:
pages 5, 31 bottom, 106–107,
109

Rugs by Polly Miller: pages 21
top, 24, 32, 70, 72, 82, 84, 88
top, 89 bottom, 150

Courtesy of Helaine and Burton
Fendelman: pages 7, 29, 86,
122–123, 163

Courtesy of Avis Skinner: pages
3, 27, 30, 44, 45, 65 top left,
96–101, 104, 105, 117, 121,
156, 164 right

Courtesy of Susan Parrish:
pages 36, 48, 62, 164 right

Courtesy of Rubens Teles:
pages 110–111, 165 center and
right, 166 left

Courtesy of Betty and Kenneth
Olsen: pages 21 bottom, 40, 49
top, 65 bottom left, 92–93, 94
bottom, 108, 112 bottom left
and top right, 113, 148, 167 left
and center

Courtesy of Richardson Gallery:
page 41

Courtesy of Barbara and Peter
Kenner: pages 94 top, 166 right

Courtesy of Grace and Elliott
Snyder: pages 14, 15, 16, 61,
116, 129, 131, 132–133

Courtesy of Art Underfoot,
Inc.: Jule Marie Smith: pages 1,
4, 6, 22–23, 52, 53, 55 right, 58
bottom, 63 bottom, 102–103,
166 center; Roslyn Logsdon:
66–67, 167 right; Fran Willey:
50–51; Tish Murphy: 33–34,
114, 127 top

Courtesy of The Tiller
Antiques: pages 115, 118 left,
130 bottom

INDEX